Tips & Tools

The Art of Experiential Group Facilitation

Jennifer Stanchfield, MS

Published by:

Wood 'N' Barnes Publishing
2717 NW 50th, Oklahoma City, OK 73112
(405) 942-6812

1st Edition © 2007, Wood 'N' Barnes Publishing, U.S.A.
All rights reserved.

This publication is sold with the understanding that the publisher is not engaged in rendering psychological, medical, or other professional services.

Cover Art by Blue Designs
Copyediting & Layout Design by Ramona Cunningham

Cover page photo, cover photo: Jeff Baird
Photos courtesy of Jeff Baird: pp. v, viii, 1, 6, 28, 34, 43, 52, 53, 57, 85, 103, 125, 135, 145
Photos courtesy of Don Morse: pp. x, 11, 18, 15, 125
Photos courtesy of Chris Harlow: pp. 9, 153
Photo courtesy of Michael Gage Peterson: pp. 76
Photo courtesy of Polly Chandler: pp. 4
Photos courtesy of Marcia Demers: pp. 36, 39
Photos courtesy of Jen Stanchfield: pp. vii, viii, 2, 3, 10, 13, 15, 17, 18, 20, 21, 23, 24, 26, 27, 29, 30, 32, 33, 37, 40, 43, 49, 50, 54, 55, 56, 58, 61,63, 64, 65, 67, 70, 71, 72, 74, 75, 77, 78, 81, 82, 87, 88, 89, 91, 92, 93, 95, 97, 99, 100, 102, 106, 107, 108, 111, 112, 114, 115, 116, 118, 119, 120, 122, 123, 130, 132, 133, 136, 138, 151, 152, 154, 164, 167
Author Photo: Paul Stanchfield

Printed in the United States of America
Oklahoma City, Oklahoma
ISBN # 978-1-885473-71-4

Foreword

As an educator with some years of adventure education experience, I was excited to read a book containing Jen's thoughts regarding what I consider to be the central practice of our profession—facilitation. I've always found her personal style to be caring and focused on searching for the value of the experience for each person and group. Reading about methods she employs to consistently translate her practices into worthy outcomes held expectant hope for me. I was not disappointed.

I really enjoyed the book for a couple of reasons. First, it is very thorough in painting a comprehensive picture of the elements to consider when doing facilitation and group work. It establishes a professional baseline of practices for newer facilitators to become thoughtful practitioners, with experience. Secondly, Jen gives pause for thought surrounding questions that a more seasoned facilitator might find useful to consider. Looking back at the notes I took when a section caught my interest, I realized that the activities presented would all be immediately useful to any practitioner. I liked them because they helped underscore a point of facilitation Jen was presenting. My list also contains many items that speak to the "art" of facilitation in the book's title. I find this appealing because it is the consideration of these ideas, and subsequent practice and implementation, that leads to those "aha" moments that are so rewarding for participants and, consequently, facilitators alike. It is those moments of connectivity that make us want to continue learning and honing our craft. It drives us to continue to practice and improve, as Jen urges in the conclusion of the book.

To summarize, this book will be valuable to a wide variety of facilitators. Its contents are well communicated. It is comprehensive in its scope, thought provoking in its depth, and user friendly with tips and suggestions for improving anyone's practice.

Mike Gessford
June 2007

Dedicated to the memory of
Evelyn Browne and Marion Beckwith
and their adventurous spirits and belief
in the power of experiential education.

Acknowledgements

Many people have contrib-
uted to this work, which
is the result of 17 years of
passionate experiential
education practice in a
variety of settings. Pam
McPhee and Kim Goody
of the University of New
Hampshire's Browne

Center were my first models of skilled experiential educators adept
at artfully guiding groups to change and grow and take ownership
of their learning.

Sandy Negley, Mauria Tanner, Jeri Claspill, Greg Smith, Patricia
Bishop, Kelly Mattingly, Amy Long, and the other talented recreational therapists at the University of Utah Neuropsychiatric Institute taught me a multitude of tools and tricks for facilitating groups
and weaving important life lessons into experiential group work in
the classroom and on the challenge course.

Dave Lockett of Stevens Point School district, Stevens Point, WI,
taught me to have an open mind and to experiment; he challenged
my preconceived notions of where and with whom experiential
education can take place, and he expanded my definitions of
group success. Donna Richter and Lynn Reining of Middleton
High School in Middleton, WI allowed me many opportunities to
co-creatively implement new ideas, activities, and methods with
students in their classrooms and challenge course program.

Jasper Hunt of Minnesota State University–Mankato reinforced
for me the value of blending theory and practice throughout one's
work. Steven Simpson of the University of Wisconsin–LaCrosse
helped me define my own philosophy of facilitation, introduced me
to the valuable lessons of Taoist philosophy, and encouraged me to
present and share my work with others in the field.

Michelle Cummings, of Training Wheels Inc., has shared my passion for promoting useful tools for experiential facilitators and has been an ideal partner in exploring opportunities and new ways to help facilitators take advantage of "teachable moments" with groups. Her energy and resourcefulness have inspired many facilitators to experiment and have fun with facilitation.

Cindi Walker, Sarah Oosterhuis, Mary Bridges, and Tom Leahy have been ongoing role models of creative, open-minded approaches to facilitation and tireless advocates for the profession of challenge course facilitator training. Jennifer Leahy has been a cheerleader and supporter of this project throughout.

The staff and clients that I worked with during my years at High 5 Adventure Learning Center who provided a great home base for practicing experiential education. Thanks to Polly Chandler, Joe Boggio, Ann Freitag, Diana Sommer and the other staff and students who gave me opportunities to explore the art of facilitation through our work together at Hinsdale, New Hampshire Middle and High School.

This book would never have come to fruition without the work of my talented, insightful editor, Mony Cunningham. She has known how to blend honest feedback with encouragement, humor, and patience. My heartfelt thanks to David Wood for believing in me and encouraging me to offer my perspectives to our field. I am proud to have worked with David, Mony, and their publishing company, whose tradition of integrity and professionalism shows in all of their work.

Finally, no words can convey my gratitude to my husband Paul, who has been willing to share space with the work I have taken home with me over the years (including the tools of the trade—rubber chickens, fleece balls, processing props—in our living room) and patiently encouraged me during the many nights, weekends, and holidays spent writing this book. He is my best critic, supporter, and partner of a lifetime!

Author's Note

The inspiration for this publication grew out of the enthusiasm
I have seen at conferences and workshops from fellow educators when engaged in sharing our favorite tools, tricks, and ideas
for working with groups. About seven years ago I was fortunate
enough to have the opportunity to start writing about some of my
own ideas and favorite tools and tips for group facilitation through
the creation of the byline "Facilitator's Toolbox" for the Association
for Challenge Course Technology's (ACCT) quarterly newsletter
Parallel Lines.

Bobby Tod of Ropeworks in Austin,
Texas created the byline "Builder's
Toolbox" and contributed articles
full of helpful tricks, tools, and ideas
for challenge course builders to
use in the field. It seemed to me
challenge course facilitators would
appreciate a similar forum focused
on the facilitation side of challenge
course practice. I started contributing to the newsletter from some
of my writings as a graduate student at Minnesota State University–Mankato and tidbits from my ongoing work with teachers and
challenge course facilitators. The efforts of Janice Gravely, Cindi
Walker, Sylvia Dresser, Holly Scott, and Adam Bondeson have en-
sured the continued publication and expansion of *Parallel Lines* as
a resource for practitioners over the past 10 years.

The "Facilitator's Toolbox" articles and the related "Toolbox Live"
workshops at ACCT's yearly conference relevant to classroom
educators, counselors, and challenge course facilitators appear in
an extended form in the following pages. For more information
on ACCT and the *Parallel Lines Newsletter* contact www.acctinfo.
org or 800-991-0286.

"The most important
attitude that can be formed
is that of the desire to go
on learning." John Dewey

Content

Introduction

Laying the Foundation

Professionals in human service and education fields work under a variety of titles: "counselor," "teacher," "therapist," "trainer," "educator." Regardless of our specific professional practice, those of us working with groups to create positive change have many commonalities. We all practice the art of facilitation, whether our aim is to empower clients to live healthier lives, aid students in learning specific skills, or resolve conflict among work teams.

> facilitate: to make easier, aid, assist, smooth the progress of, to make possible, to make easier, create, compose.

The word "facilitate" is used in a variety of fields to describe the process of guiding, helping, assisting, and creating. Experiential facilitation is an intentional approach to facilitation based on the idea that people learn and change more from the process of working through problems and finding solutions than from being given answers and solutions by a teacher/counselor/leader. In the context of this book, I use "facilitator" to describe the role of a person in the field of education, counseling, corporate training, or other related area who works to help individuals and groups create positive change, learn new skills, and gain new perspectives.

During my years as an educator, recreational therapist, and challenge course facilitator, I worked with groups of all ages and backgrounds in many different settings. Through the blend of these experiences as a practitioner and my formal training in the theories of education, cognitive psychology, recreational therapy, and experiential education, two consistent themes have emerged as a basis for approaching facilitation: the philosophy of **experiential education** and the notion of **participant-centered facilitation** or guiding a group. These concepts are the underlying foundations of the activities, ideas, and strategies for facilitation that are presented throughout this book.

Group Snapshots

Snapshot 1

Elementary students stand in a circle looking with rapt attention at two high school students demonstrating how to play a cooperative tag game, Giants, Wizards & Elves. Teachers on the sidelines comment: "I have never seen this group so focused! I am so excited to see Karen participating; she usually sits on the sidelines!" "Can you believe Michelle is LEADING today? She used to be the shyest student in my class!"

Snapshot 2

Professionals from a medical equipment company gather around a table putting together pieces from the group puzzle they created. The pieces represent each person's role and contribution to the organization. We hear: "John's willingness to let us to do our jobs balanced with his availability makes me feel trusted, like I'm an important part of our team." "Jane helps us see the big picture and keep our perspective when things start feeling out of control."

Snapshot 3

Families with adolescents in a treatment program attend family ropes night on the challenge course. An adolescent girl reaches out to help her mother cross the wire cable, encouraging her, "You can trust me!" The group enthusiastically claps and cheers as this pair completes the difficult challenge together, knowing that  they have struggled with communication and trust and are now demonstrating some of the positive changes the group has worked toward.

The Experiential Approach

The experiential approach is based on the idea that change and growth take place when people are actively (physically, socially, intellectually, emotionally) involved in their learning rather than just being receivers of information. The philosophy of experiential education was promoted by John Dewey, an educator and philosopher in the early 20th century who was one of many innovators during the Progressive Movement in education.* He and others of the Progressive Movement felt a time-honored and common-sense

---

* A movement in education, societal reform, and the arts in both Europe and North America during the late 19th century and early 20th century. This movement was a reaction to what many believed was the narrowness and formalism of traditional education and the new ideals of industry and modern society. A main objective of the progressive movement in schools was to educate the "whole person" to focus on people's physical and emotional as well as intellectual growth. Creative and vocational arts increased in importance in the curriculum, and learners were encouraged toward experimentation and independent thinking. Progressive educational ideas and practices were most powerfully advanced in the U.S. by John Dewey. This movement faded in popularity after World War II but left lasting institutions such as Montessori Schools, vocational education, and the field of experiential education.

belief was being forgotten in modern education: that people learn most when they are actively involved in their learning and find the material relevant and attractive in some way. He emphasized that learners need to feel a sense of control over the learning situation and should be provided with opportunities to reflect on the learning experiences so they relate, connect, and transfer to real life and future learning. As John Dewey stated, "The most important attitude that can be formed is that of the desire to go on learning."

Experiential facilitators engage groups in activities that give participants opportunities to take ownership of their learning. They create situations that allow learners to actively explore and practice concepts they are learning and facilitate the practice of reflection on how these lessons relate to the learners, current and future real-life situations.

What I find especially exciting about the philosophy of experiential education is that the theories John Dewey and other progressive educators put forward almost a century ago are being validated today by current studies of the brain and how people learn. In the past few decades, new technologies such as brain imaging

"Good leaders make people feel that they're at the very heart of things, not at the periphery. Everyone feels that he or she makes a difference to the success of the organization. When that happens people feel centered and that gives their work meaning." Warren Bennis

have become available to study the living human brain and how it works. Neuroscientists have been able to identify optimal conditions for learning. This information has translated into theories that educators call "brain-based" learning (Jensen, 1998). Brain-based theory emphasizes many of the same tenets John Dewey did so long ago, especially the value of combining physical action and reflection in learning, giving learners choice and control over their learning (Jensen, 2000) and involving the components of challenge, novelty, choice, feedback, social interaction, and active participation in the learning environment (Diamond & Hobson, 1998).

Principles of Experiential Education

- The learner is a participant in learning rather than a receiver of information.

- More can be learned through struggling with a problem than by being provided with the solution.

- Experiential learning or therapy is active, not necessarily physical, but active. Learners actively engage in solving problems by using creativity, posing questions, interacting with others, experimenting, taking responsibility for themselves and others, and finding meaning in their experiences.

- The learner needs to feel intrinsically motivated to learn.

- Learners must perceive internal freedom and independence—making choices about experiences, taking responsibility in experiences, and feeling in control of their learning (Dewey, 1938).

- Relevancy is imperative—lessons and concepts must feel relevant and meaningful to the learner. Lessons need to have intrinsic value and relate to real life, in both the present and future situations.

- Participants must have time to reflect. Reflection involves thoughtful time connecting the experience to real-life situations. As learners practice reflective skills, they develop insight—a skill that will help them in many areas of their lives.

- Experiences should be carefully chosen to meet the needs and differing styles of the learners. This requires creativity, flexibility, and intention from the facilitator.

- Facilitators use metaphors to help learners retain and connect lessons, and they create opportunities to reflect on or process experiences to increase meaning and relevance and help the learner transfer these skills to other parts of their life.

- Facilitators encourage spontaneous learning; participants may take lessons in many different directions. Good facilitators "go with the flow" and move with the lessons the group is creating.

- Facilitators structure appropriate experiences, but they must be flexible, acting as a guide and role model. A facilitator initiates learning; the participant takes it from there.

- Learners thrive when they are in an environment where they feel valued, respected, and supported.

- An atmosphere of fun will help open doors to learning. Learners can practice communication, cooperation, trust, problem-solving, and insight in a milieu of fun.

- Facilitators effectively sequence lessons so they can be built upon each other. John Dewey stated that one can learn from any and all experiences, but growth through experience must create conditions for future growth.

"A leader is best when people barely know he exists, not so good when people obey and acclaim him, worse when they despise him.... But of a good leader who talks little when his work is done, his aim fulfilled, they will say, 'We did it ourselves.'" Lao Tzu

Guiding Your Group

The basic tenet of experiential education is the idea of facilitators (e.g., teachers, leaders) approaching their work as guides in the process of discovery, rather than as all-knowing teachers and centers of knowledge and direction. As I gain experience as a facilitator, I realize my effectiveness actually increases when I step back and allow group members to take more control in the learning and teaching process. With experience, I've become more comfortable taking a less directive approach and trusting in a naturally unfolding group process; I've come to embrace the idea of "participant-centered facilitation."

Steven Simpson of the University of Wisconsin–LaCrosse, an author and practitioner in the field of experiential education, coined this term in his work connecting the field of experiential education and Taoist philosophy.* In the participant-centered approach, the facilitator aims to gradually shift responsibility for the success of the experience from him/herself to the participants. As the group progresses and the facilitator fades into the background, group members take more ownership and control over their learning.

Principles of Participant-Centered Facilitation

- Facilitators encourage spontaneous learning; participants may take lessons in many different directions. "Go with the flow" and move with the lessons the group is creating.

- Facilitators structure appropriate experiences but remain flexible, acting as guide and role model. Facilitators initiate learning; participants take it from there.

- Learners should feel fully valued, respected, and supported.

---

* Steven Simpson, Ph.D., is the author of *The Leader Who is Hardly Known: Self-less Teaching In the Chinese Tradition*, 2003, and *The Processing Pinnacle: An Educator's Guide to Better Processing*, 2006, both published by Wood 'N' Barnes Publishing.

- Participants' choice and control is essential. Empowering participants to say no and to set reasonable parameters around their participation creates an atmosphere of healthy trust and increases involvement from reluctant participants.

- Participants should be allowed to pass during group discussions. This empowers them to have control over their learning and practice sharing at their own pace. When participants are given the power to pass, they learn to trust the facilitator and group and often end up offering a great deal to the group at their own pace.

- Facilitators aiming to create change by pushing comfort zones should be aware of the fine balance between a positive challenge and a potentially damaging experience.

- Participants may take activities and lessons somewhere different from what you had in mind. Be prepared to learn something new! Be aware that you might have to artfully help them navigate back to the present moment in order to meet the group needs.

- Facilitators should try to direct questions back to the group, letting participants help each other.

- Facilitators should be prepared for the unexpected and welcome the opportunities that arise when group work goes differently than planned. Be willing to let go of your agenda to meet the needs of the group.

This book offers concrete examples of participant-centered facilitation. In sharing some of my favorite methods, activities, and approaches, I hope to give readers some valuable tools for implementing experiential education. Each chapter takes readers through some of the specific steps and strategies I consistently find successful in guiding learners through the process of group development learning and reflection.

Working with groups of people as an educator and guide is a rewarding and exciting occupation. It also demands a great deal of creative output, novelty, and energy on the part of the practitioner. Facilitators gain skills through a combination of practice, observation, and theory. Good facilitators never stop developing and refining their style and searching for new aspects and tools to inform their work with groups. This book is intended to be just such a resource and tool for experiential group facilitators of all levels of experience who are looking to spark their creativity, gain new perspectives on their work, and find new ideas to support the process of individual and group development. It is my hope that readers find this blend of theory and concrete tips and tools will enhance their practice of facilitation and inspire their own unique style.

"Leadership should be more participative than directive, more enabling than performing."
Mary D. Poole

Chapter 1

Setting the Tone: Creating a Positive Environment for Learning

One of the most fundamental aspects of effective group programming is taking the time to help participants create a positive, supportive environment in which they can share and work together. It can be risky for people to try new activities and share their ideas, reactions, and opinions in a group. Research on the brain and learning suggests that learners participate in activities and retain lessons more readily when they feel safe and supported in their learning environment (Jensen, 2000). So be intentional about how, when, and where you engage group members from the very start of a program.

Time spent up front consciously and carefully planning activities that build a group's comfort level will pay off later. Allow groups to explore the novelty of experiential group work with a sense of ownership and control. Participants need to feel that the activities they are participating in or the materials they are learning are useful and relevant to their goals. Effective facilitators start this process before groups even walk through the door.

Recipe for Building a Positive Group Environment

Facilitation is like cooking. When you first start cooking, you follow the tried and true recipes from family, a friend or colleague, or a cookbook. As your skills increase, you start to improvise and vary the ingredients. Successful facilitators vary ingredients all the time to keep things interesting or to "spice up" their group work, but they always keep in mind the key ingredients that make it happen. There is a lot of room for creativity, style, and adaptation in cooking, but key rules and ingredients are needed in order for a cake to rise or a sauce to thicken. Facilitators must balance the parameters of the situation, the needs of the group, and their own creativity and style.

Key Ingredients for Creating Positive Learning Environments

More ideas on each of these topics will be addressed throughout this book.

- Start off with style! Introductory activities set the tone for the program and future group interaction. Think carefully about appropriate beginning activities that include introductions, "breaking the ice," and goal setting. Take time for this process. Sharing commonalities builds trust and empathy. When people are given an opportunity to share with each other in a comfortable way, they build the capacity to go more in-depth later in group development.

- Create an opportunity for people to meet and greet in a non-threatening, conversational, fun way to help dispel fears about group process or being "put on the spot."

- Help group members know and use names in order to build trust and positive communication and establish a supportive environment. A person's name is very important to them. Presenting a series of activities that help members use and practice the names of others can be very helpful to the forming stage of group development.

- Keep an eye on time parameters and plan accordingly. It takes time to sequence and build healthy trust between group members and between facilitator and group members. Time and experience together can build comfort in sharing thoughts, ideas, and feelings. Set aside time for the reflective aspect of learning. Be patient with the group development pace. Time spent up front building trust and quality reflective skills pays off later!

- Consider the physical environment when planning or evaluating group experience. Intentionally select the environment; arrange seating based on the goals and needs of the group.

- There should be an opportunity for participants and facilitator to share their clear expectations and goals for the program.

- Participant choice and control is essential. Empowering participants to say "no" and setting reasonable parameters around their participation creates an atmosphere of healthy trust and will actually increase involvement from reluctant participants. In group work, facilitators often aim to create change by pushing comfort zones and creating disequilibrium. But there is a fine line between positive disequilibrium and a miseducative or potentially damaging experience.

- Group norms about desired behaviors should be created by participants after they have spent some time together. They should be reflected upon and revisited throughout a program.

- Thoughtfully sequence activities to build the capacity of trust over time (time means something different in relevant terms for a one-day program than a year-long program).

- Differing learning styles and needs of participants should be taken into consideration.

- Reflection, regularly checking in, and reviewing are integral to group process, so that experiences can be built upon one another and related to real life and future learning.

Creating a positive environment for learning in group is an ongoing process that takes commitment, perseverance, and often "strength of heart" from the facilitator. The effort is well worth it in the end.

A few years ago, I had the opportunity to coteach two semester-long challenge course classes with two different teachers. The physical educator I taught the first class with spent a great deal of time during the first two weeks engaging students in name activities, trust building, reflection, and group norms agreements. The second teacher chose to spend only a few sessions on ice breaking and warm-up. The group norms agreement was entirely skipped over in the second class, and they delved right into challenge course activities, spending very little time on reflection.

The principal and other teachers visited the two classes throughout the semester. More importantly, the coteachers of the classes visited each other's classes. The difference in the dynamics of the two classes was repeatedly commented upon by those observers. It was noted that the class that spent time up front creating a positive environment sequentially, including name activities, ice breaking, an involved trust sequence, and regular reflection was

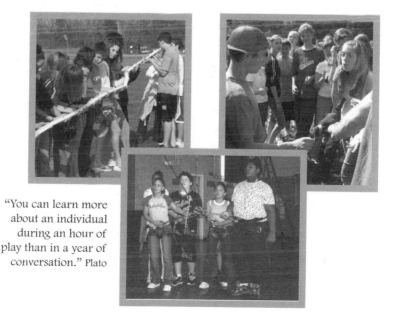

"You can learn more about an individual during an hour of play than in a year of conversation." Plato

two weeks ahead of the other class in course content and technical skills, despite having spent more time on the group building activities. As a result of the feedback and positive outcome, the second teacher asked to meet with the first teacher for input on adding to the warm-up activities and reflection for the next semester's course.

Students' comments show how the time spent in a positive group environment increased their perceptions of an overall positive school climate:

> "I think our class has become more of a family group, always helping out and supporting others."

> "Our class as a group has changed dramatically. At first no one felt comfortable working together. By the end we had pulled together as one problem-solving unit."

> "Sometimes it is really challenging working in a group. I usually don't have to rely on other people to get things done, but this class is forcing me to work on that."

> "Nick and I were practicing tying knots in phys-ed class today. We had fun both working and joking around. I really like that aspect of this class. We really have a bond that allows us to laugh and play, work and think together. And I think that is really special."

> "I am getting to know people better, and I can actually say hi to them when before I didn't have a clue who they were. And to me, there is meaning behind the hello instead of a hello that means absolutely nothing."

Individuals are often less willing to share and participate fully in groups that have not built a trustworthy community. When the facilitator and group take the time to focus on building community, developing trust, and defining positive group norms, the group performs better and takes learning further. When this kind of time and thoughtful effort is not taken, the group often functions on a superficial or even dysfunctional level, achieving less together. Although many of us are pressured by external time restraints and the expectation to move quickly through group activities, making the time up front to establish a positive environment within the group will pay off later!

The Power of Play—Don't Be Afraid to Have Fun!

A couple of years ago I was asked to present a challenge course program for a group of executives from a bio-technology company. As with many corporate programs, the staff development contact from the corporation wanted a detailed description of each activity I had planned, was nervous about anything that might be too "touchy feely," and expressed the desire to avoid too much of that "silly name game stuff."

When the group arrived, we engaged in a series of activities to start the day, including Handshake Mingle and Have You Ever? (described in the following pages). The executives enthusiastically participated. The contact person I had coordinated with was there in the midst of it all playfully interacting with his team. I heard one man gleefully saying "This is fun!" to another participant in the Have You Ever? game. They seemed to appreciate the opportunity to let go and have fun together in this way.

I believe this worked and was not perceived as "that silly name game stuff" because we carefully sequenced these activities, starting with partner-type activities first. We made opportunities for people to get warmed up and have some choices in their participation (e.g., having the opportunity to take an "out" from being in the middle in Have You Ever?). We were conscious of not putting pressure on those who weren't quite ready to engage that way. We blended just the "right amount" of playful, interactive, large group games, partner sharing, and then intriguing problem solving.

Recently a local mental health agency asked me and a colleague to run an afternoon of experiential team building activities as part of its annual fall staff development week. These 80 professionals worked in different aspects of the agency and within a few local communities. The staff development days also involved a great deal of lecture time.

We started the group with some of the activities mentioned in this chapter (e.g., Handshake Mingle). At the end of the afternoon a woman came up to me, looking very serious, and said, "There is something I need to tell you." My immediate thought was that she was uncomfortable with something we had done and wanted to express her concern. Instead she said, "I want to let you know how much I appreciated that partner handshake activity. Every year we get together and have to sit through these lectures. I see these people who work for the agency every year, but I don't get to connect with them or even know their names. This year I got to do that for the first time! I now have a connection with my ankle shake partner, Bill. We know each other's name, and made a connection. I just wanted to let you know how much I appreciate that!"

For the past four years, I have been working with teachers, community members, and students in a rural New England town. Many people in this small community face a variety of socioeconomic and environmental stressors; their school is overcrowded and was named a "failing school." I was excited to take part in a grant aimed at improving these conditions by strengthening the learning community in the school and connecting with prevention efforts in the community.

We started the program with classroom-based, team building initiatives and games, and followed up with a series of challenge course experiences. When I first attended one of the 8th grade classes, the students were almost hostile. They were very disruptive and inattentive. Put-downs were flying around the room. During that first day, I saw one student tease another to the point of tears. Throughout the next few months, we persisted in involving students in group building activities, reflection, and group norms activities. We used a great deal of praise, positive reinforcement, and choice throughout the process.

The following spring during a school trip to a challenge course, I snapped a picture of those same two students—the one who had been dishing out the mean comments and relentlessly teasing that first day was now reaching out her hand to help that same peer walk across a wiggling cable. Back at school, teachers reported that students were more willing to ask a peer in a positive way to stop negative behavior in the classroom. Students were able to identify the positive changes that had taken place in their classroom community.

Teachers noticed the changes in their students:

"Kids are asking other kids to be focused and doing it in a nicer way; it's peer pressure in a nice way; I've not seen this happen in all my years of teaching."

"In the beginning kids separated into small groups or isolated themselves. Now they are more accepting of kids that were not part of the 'in group.'"

"I have seen a very distinct change in regards to their ability to talk, share, and take charge.

"Students are definitely beginning to problem solve better and especially listen to each other better during the process. They are accepting more responsibility for each other."

The Physical Environment

The Circle

Circles are a symbol of wholeness. When a group forms a circle everyone in the group can see everyone else. In creating a circle, a group creates a physical communal space, where everyone is on equal footing with equal responsibility. Circular seating or standing arrangements are effective when first meeting a group, giving directions, having a group discussion, or using a processing tool.

I have come to believe that the most effective classroom design is to arrange desks in a circle or semi-circle. This way the teacher and students see everyone. A student who is struggling can't

"disappear" in the back of the room. With no space for covert behaviors, students are more able to take responsibility for engaging in prosocial behaviors and participating in class discussion. This approach is common to therapeutic settings for the same reasons mentioned above, and it is also beneficial in adult learning situations such as college classrooms or corporate training.

Many people are not accustomed to forming circles as a group. Most of society's group forums, such as schools, theatres, churches, and town halls, are traditionally set up in rows. It's a good idea to explain to the group why you are asking them to form circles for activity and dialogue. With children it might take practice to get comfortable forming circles for group interaction. Eventually, however, it will become second nature to form a circle when they come together to talk. I noticed this change in groups I have been involved with over longer periods of time. The group of students I have worked with over the past few years, in a long-term grant program, initially needed a good deal of prompting and reinforcement to form a circle. Now, they automatically form one when we start our program without my asking, and they spontaneously circle up without prompting when they recognize they need to share or plan together.

Think about setting up problem-solving activities in a circular space instead of a linear one so that group members must face each other during conflict situations. Many of the group games and activities also involve a circular space. I often take a warm-up activity or initiative that has traditionally been used in a field or gym space and I adapt it to a smaller circular space. This adaptation brings the group together both physically and mentally, helping them become centered and focused on their experiences together.

The Classroom or Boardroom

Though challenge courses and group work in a novel outdoor or retreat setting can be a great experience for everyone involved, I have found that the group's own classroom or boardroom can be just as novel a setting for creating engaging group experiences and

"The most extraordinary thing about really good teachers is that they transcend accepted educational methods."
Margaret Mead

lessons that transfer to everyday life. Even a cramped classroom can be a space where very positive change happens. When we move the chairs aside in a classroom and the group participates in fun activities with a lesson or purpose, I notice that participants seem to be able to transfer the lesson part of an activity nicely to what goes on day to day in the classroom or workplace. When people are taken away from their usual working space, the "field trip" or "day off" mentality can sometimes get in the way of applying lessons learned to daily situations.

By creating community building experiences right in the classroom or boardroom, participants increase their positive feelings, associations, and identity with that space and what happens there. This leads to future possibilities for positive change and growth to happen in that classroom space.

This is especially relevant for short-term group work, early on team building activities, and interventions with a group. With groups involved in ongoing facilitation, an experience in a novel environment at the right time enhances the group's capacity for positive change. The novelty "ups the ante" for focus, responsibility, and challenge that can then transfer back to the classroom or boardroom. The ideal situation is a balance of experiential-based community building activities facilitated both in the classroom setting and off site in a novel setting.

Outdoors

Facilitating outdoors is fundamental to many types of programming, from expeditionary learning to challenge course experiences. The novelty of being outdoors in a beautiful setting can deeply enrich group experience and engagement. Taking a group somewhere out of its standard frame of reference can be very positive when strategically planned at the right time. The novelty of the new setting helps group members remember the experience.

The outdoor environment can also pose challenges to group focus. Issues such as comfortable seating, weather, or noise can be very distracting. Some participants can be intimidated by the outdoor setting at first. I have worked with students from urban areas who were nervous about being out in the woods at a challenge course site and very distracted by aspects of the natural setting such as insects. Despite the distractions, it was obviously beneficial in many ways to experience the outdoors.

Every physical setting has its pros and cons. I recommend that facilitators just be conscious of the learning environment they are creating and pay attention to the differences in the participation in

"You will find more in the woods than in books. Trees and stones will teach you that which you can never learn from masters." Saint Bernard

each setting. This conscious observation on your part as facilitator will help with successful sequencing of activities. Be thoughtful about the requirements of each activity setting, and be aware that participants' comfort levels with being outdoors can differ greatly from your own. Designing aids such as carpet squares or a tarp for sitting on wet ground or hot chocolate on a cold day can be very helpful. This attention and planning can mitigate potential negative aspects of facilitating in the outdoors and can enhance great opportunities that arise from working in a natural setting.

Starting With Style

Introductory activities create a positive environment, enhance performance, and set the tone for the rest of the program. Taking time up front for the group to get comfortable and learn names will pay off later. The more I work with groups, I realize how powerful some of the simpler things we do as facilitators can be. An engaging opening activity designed to get the group interacting and sharing names, backgrounds, and goals in an intriguing way can really maximize the outcome of group process.

Every facilitator has his or her own set of favorite opening activities. Many activity books have whole sections on this subject. I have learned some of the best and most effective activities in my repertoire from other facilitators and through experimenting with groups and adapting activities over time and experience. The following are a few favorites that work to set the tone for most group situations.

Postcard/Object Introductions

Collecting postcards is a hobby I have long enjoyed, and I often use them as a reflective tool (see A Teachable Moment, 2005). Using postcards or objects can also be a fun and engaging method to catch the interest of a group as they enter a program. Often when a group is coming together, the first moments of gathering can feel awkward. In conference and training programs participants often arrive at different times. For a workshop that is scheduled to begin at 9:00 some arrive at 8:30 and some at 9:15. Having a casual activity to draw a group in and help "fill" that potentially awkward time not only helps the facilitator feel more comfortable with that "down" time but actually ends up becoming an opportunity for participants to create connections with each other. The participants start to switch their focus from everything happening outside of the workshop or classroom experience to becoming fully present at the workshop or program.

I was first introduced to an activity using objects for introductions as a student at UNH taking a challenge course management class. Our course instructors Pam McPhee and Kim Goody invited participants to find something in our pockets or back packs and share it with a partner. They encouraged us to share an object that had an amusing or interesting story about it, share that story, and share a little about ourselves with our partners. We then temporarily traded objects with our partners, and introduced each other to the whole group.

This worked really well in a college course for adventure educators, as the class was made up of many extroverts who were already quite comfortable with group process. I really enjoyed the activity and the associations and interesting conversations that came out of the discussions of the personal objects. As you can imagine, I did not get quite the same response when I tried the activity in the same way with other kinds of groups such as adolescents in the treatment program where I worked, or teachers coming in at 8 a.m. for a staff development program. They often found it daunting to share something so personal. So I started bringing my own assortment of objects in a "treasure chest" (see page 99) or my "postcard kit." I lay them out on a table and ask participants to choose an object/postcard that represents their mood, a goal for the program, a strength they bring to the group, or some other theme that fits the group. I not only use activities like this for the first day of school, camp, or training program; but also after certain milestones, like the New Year, or as reflection at the end of a unit in class.

Recent research about the brain and learning suggests that when learners can attach thoughts/key concepts to a metaphoric image they may retain it longer. Often people find it easier to share when they can attach their thoughts to an object or image, and conversation and reflection can become more metaphorically rich than with conversation alone. This method is "participant-centered" as it puts more control on the students/learners for interpreting their experience/feelings/goals rather than the teacher/leader directing and possibly inserting his or her own interpretation or agenda.

Postcard/Object Introductions

The novelty of the cards/objects and sharing information with partners rather than answering individually feels less intimidating than some other introductory activities. I also get a pulse on my group and glean their attitudes and expectations for the group experience.

Facilitation Suggestion:

- Spread postcards/objects on a table or floor where they are accessible to all group members.

- Ask group members to choose a card/object that represents one of the following:
  - The reason you came today
  - Goals or expectations for the program
  - Strengths you bring to the group

  Or in a classroom situations, you give the following prompt:
  - Choose a card that represents what your summer break was like.

- Have participants find a partner and share their card/object and information about themselves.

- Give them an opportunity to introduce each other and their chosen cards/objects to the group.

- If the group is large, mix warm-up activities with the sharing. For example, ask two or three sets of partners to share, then play a name game, have two or three more sets of introductions, then another icebreaker, etc.

Handshake Mingle

This has become my favorite icebreaker activity and a main staple of my repertoire. I learned this game from Aimee Desrosier Cochran who used this activity during her time at Springfield College's Challenge Course program. It gives participants of all ages and backgrounds an opportunity to warm up and

interact in a non-threatening way. The beauty of this activity is that it is energizing and fun and everyone gets a chance to come face to face with someone new and do a brief introduction. I recommend this activity for groups where you want to break up cliques and facilitate group interaction with everyone. This can be especially helpful in classroom settings.

Facilitation Suggestions:

- Have everyone find a partner.

- Ask the group members to give their partner a "high 5." Tell participants these are now their high 5 partners.

- Next ask them to find new partners and give each other a low five. These are their low 5 partners.

- Now have them find their high 5 partners again (give them a high 5), then find their low 5 partners again (give them a low 5).

- Next ask them to find new partners, face them, and give them an ankle shake (lean over, bending at the knees, and shake their partner's ankle). These are their ankle shake partners. Start the sequence again: find their high 5, then low 5, then ankle shake partners.

- Continue this sequence adding new partner activities as appropriate (e.g., a "fishing partner"—one is the reel and one the fish). You will witness laughter, positive interaction, and fun. Participants really will remember each other.

- Later, you can use the partners to form groups or have them run through this sequence to say goodbye to their partners as a closing at the end of the day.

I sometimes insert "get to know you" questions into this activity. For example, after reeling in their "fishing partner," I have participants share a fishing story. Almost everyone has a fishing story, and if they don't, they can make one up just like any good fisherman.

Participants tend to remember their partners from Handshake Mingle and share that connection throughout the remainder of the program and beyond. You can utilize this initial partner connection later in the program when you want to divide into partners again for an activity or reflection. Ask group members to find their "high 5 partner" or their "fishing partner." You will be surprised how well they remember who that person was, sometimes even days later.

To close the program, invite participants to revisit this activity and share, reflect on, and/or celebrate aspects of their experience and say goodbye to each of their original partners. At the end of the day, I sometimes use metaphor and have participants find their high 5 partner and share something they are proud of from the day or experience. I then have them find their fishing partner and share a key learning they "caught" or will take away from the program or experience, and so on.

Facilitating this kind of activity can be kept interesting for participants and yourself by exploring and experimenting with new twists. For example, try new handshake/greeting variations based on comments from group members or popular culture. I was inspired to use "rock on partners" after watching a documentary on the heavy metal band Metallica. I asked if there were any heavy metal fans in the group and then asked them to show the group how to greet their partners with "heavy metal horns" and "rock on."

Recently my husband bought a motorcycle. After a ride, he asked if I knew the sign for "pop a wheelie." He shared that he was given the "pop a wheelie" sign by a kid and proceeded to show me the sign. The next day, I started using "pop a wheelie" greetings. So far at least one person has volunteered to share his/her version of the "pop a wheelie" sign in every group.

Have fun mixing up your methods. If you aren't comfortable facilitating "silly" greetings with a more solemn group, just have partners mix with simple greetings and "get to know you" questions. Concentric circles is a more subdued version of Handshake Mingle that has a similar outcome.

"To be playful and serious at the same time is possible, in fact it defines the ideal mental condition."
John Dewey

Concentric Circles

This introductory activity can also be used as a reflective and closing activity (Cain, Cummings, & Stanchfield, 2005). It has been a staple activity in my repertoire since I first picked it up from Paul Hutchinson at MSU–Mankato. It is fairly non-intimidating with participants conversing with only one other person at a time. This activity can be adapted to most age or size groups. It works especially well with large groups.

Facilitation Suggestions:

- Divide the group in half, and have them form two circles with the participants facing each other in an inner circle and an outer circle.

- Ask participants to greet each other by name and have them participate in a cooperative activity together such as "finger fencing," "gotcha," or "partner, one-handed shoe tying" (see Karl Rohnke's *Funn Stuff* for creative partner activities).

- After completing the activity, ask participants to share their answers to a "get to know you" question asked by the facilitator (e.g., What is the most unusual food you have ever eaten? What was your favorite vaca- tion? What do you want to get out of today's program?).

- After a few moments of conversation, invite the inner circle to form new partners by moving four spaces to the left, greeting the other participants they pass. Ask the new partners to greet each other, provide another cooperative activity, and another question to discuss.

- The activity continues with alternating movement between the inside and outside circle, followed by activities and questions.

Importance of Names

A key ingredient for creating a positive environment is to help group members know and use each other's names  from the very beginning of a program. Even in settings where you would assume people know each other's names already, they actually don't, or sometimes with youth programs, are not using and honoring each other's names in a respectful way. Name activities can help groups not only practice names but explore the concepts of connecting with others, honoring individual strengths and personalities, and showing respect.

As you present the icebreakers previously mentioned you can weave in reminders for participants to share and repeat their names as they visit each partner in the Handshake Mingle or Concentric Circles. It can also be helpful to have some engaging name activities in your repertoire. I have a few favorites that involve groups in a playful and non-threatening way.

Name Roulette

I learned this kinesthetic activity from my colleagues Jim Grout and Karl Rohnke (Rohnke & Grout, 1998).

Facilitation Suggestions:

- Divide participants into two groups and have them form side-by-side circles.

- Place an object between the two circles that acts as a marker.

- Have both circles of participants shuffle left or right while facing the center of their circles—no looking over their shoulder.

- When you say stop, the two participants who are at the marker have to turn around and name the person they are now facing. Whoever names the other person first captures that person onto their team, and the captive must join that circle.

The value in this activity is that when presented with the challenge, participants will study up on each other's names. Give teams a few minutes at the start to review the other team's names together.

Peek a Who

Another favorite, often called "Peek a Who" (Rohnke, 1991), is similar to name roulette but adds the intrigue of hiding behind a blanket. I've used this activity primarily with elementary students, but I'm finding that both adults and adolescents also enjoy the playful, hiding aspect.

Facilitation Suggestions:

- Have two facilitators or group members hold up a large blanket.

- Divide the group into two teams and have them stand on opposite sides of the blanket, hidden from the view of the other team.

- Each team then chooses one person to move up close to the blanket.

- On the count of three, the blanket drops and the two participants race to name each other.

- The winner captures that person onto their team.

I often use a variation of this game with groups that either know each other or have been learning about each other. The following version practices compliments and celebrating individual strengths.

- In this version, the two players behind the blanket sit back to back.

- When the blanket is dropped, their teammates describe the person from the other team to their teammate, who tries to guess who is behind them.

- Encourage participants to use positive, non-physical characteristics about the person they are describing (i.e., "she is very creative," "he is good in math," "she climbed Mt. Washington last week," "she was the leader of the last group challenge").

Name Meanings

When people have more information to associate with a person's name, it helps them make a stronger connection and better remember that name. I recently learned a simple but very effective activity from a group of teachers in Laconia, NH. Many facilitators use group "line-up" challenges. This version of the Name Line-Up adds some interest and depth to this common activity.

Facilitation Suggestions:

- Simply ask the group to line up silently by the number of letters in their name, or preferred nickname.

- Once the group is successful, have them go around and share their name and what they know about its origin, i.e., whether it is a family name, or what they know about its meaning.

This activity is a particular favorite because groups find it interesting and fun, and it helps participants learn more about each other and make associations that help them remember other group members' names.

Goals, Expectations, and Boundaries

The aforementioned activities are not only used for introductions, but also for group members to communicate their goals or expectations of the program. The Postcard/Object Introductions activity can be used quite effectively for goal setting. Using these activities to articulate goals helps the facilitator and group members tailor activities to meet the needs of the group and appropriately order and choose activities and interventions. Another successful engaging activity for helping group members articulate their goals, expectations, and/or attitudes uses campaign buttons.

Button for the Day

This fun activity was inspired by a shopping trip with a friend to a local novelty store. Jen Ottinger and I were gathering postcards and charms for my processing tool kit. Jen spotted a campaign button display that included an assortment of buttons depicting a variety of different words, clever slogans and symbols ranging from yin yang and peace signs to lightning bolts. Some had phrases such as "trust me" or "cleverly disguised as a responsible adult." Jen suggested that I "do something with those buttons," and inspired me to create one of my favorite introduction and reflection activities. The next day we used the buttons at our staff retreat. It was a great success as an icebreaker and for setting our goals for the day. Later we used the buttons as a reflection tool, referring back to the buttons we initially chose as we recognized our progress throughout our meeting.

Facilitation Suggestions:

- Place an assortment of buttons with a variety of appropriate slogans and symbols in a space where all group members have access to them. It is helpful to have a large enough selection for group members to feel they have a choice.

- Ask participants to choose a button that represents their mood or the attitude, quality, or strength they are bringing to the day.

- Depending on the size or goals of the group, have participants choose partners and share as in the Object Trade activity, or go around in a circle and ask group members to share individually (always allow group members to pass).

- Allowing participants to wear the buttons for the day can inspire interesting conversation and add a sense of fun and camaraderie.

- At the end of the day or program, use them in closing to report on any changes in attitudes, strengths, etc.

Along with giving participants an opportunity to share some of their goals for a program, the facilitator needs to set any necessary expectations or ground rules for the group. Front loading expectations and ideas for the group to think about at the start of the program can be effectively done in a fun, short, interactive way. There should be a difference between the program/facilitator-driven ground rules communicated at the start of a program and the group norms or value agreements created by group members themselves later in the group process. It is after the group has experienced some time working together—seeing and experiencing the strengths and weaknesses and actually experiencing some conflict or struggle—that creating their own norms will become most valuable. For more information and ideas about engaging groups in the process of creating group norms, see pages 56 through 69.

Chapter 2

Designing the Experience:
Sequencing Group Activities

Be thoughtful, observant, and intentional in your planning, presentation, and evaluation of activities with groups. Many in the
education field refer to this conscious and deliberate ordering of
activities as sequencing. The intention of sequencing is to maximize learning opportunities and the emotional and physical safety
of the group. It is one of the most important aspects of effective
facilitation of group work.

> sequencing: the careful ordering of group activities
> based on the group's needs, goals, and setting.

There is no correct method or specific model for sequencing programs. Approach sequencing as a dynamic process that takes into
careful consideration the group's goals and agenda, participants'
emotional and physical safety, the personality and dynamics of the
group, available activities, allotted time, and the physical environment.

Effective facilitators pay attention to the group development process
and allow time for trust building. It is important to balance the level
of the activity and/or challenge presented with the participants' abilities to meet the challenge or activity. Group leaders need to observe
their group continually in order to be sure the activities they select fit
the needs and goals of the group and the specific situation.

The time needed for participants to create relationships and build trust is different for every group. When this connection and sense of community are developed, groups will take learning further and get more benefit out of the group activities they engage in. Allow time for this to happen by choosing activities that build upon each other.

Be sensitive to the time of day, physical comfort, and attention span of participants when sequencing activities. As a facilitator, being flexible in dealing with the unexpected is key. Listen to your group and be prepared to change your plan midstream in order to adapt to the ever-changing needs of the group and to take advantage of new opportunities for learning that emerge as a group works together.

Even when working with groups with similar characteristics, in the same setting, with the same program goals, the actual lesson plan changes with each group in response to its emerging unique personality and needs. Every group has a different personality and participates in activities in different ways. In my classroom facilitation experiences and in leading challenge course and facilitation training workshops, individual class/group participation and accomplishments were different even though the topic areas were consistent and planned activities were similar with each group.

Activities you carefully plan prior to a workshop or group session may be specifically relevant for one group's personality and needs but not another's. This is one of the exciting aspects of group facilitation. There is great variety in group experience and varying opportunities to take advantage of teachable moments. With experience, facilitators develop the art of reading their group and adjusting activities in a creative way throughout group process to move learning and change forward.

Careful sequencing maximizes participation by allowing people to engage at a pace that works for them. Experiential group work can be very powerful. If groups are ready to engage in the process great things can occur. Conversely, if a group is not emotionally or physically ready to encounter certain "learning adventures," the experience could be damaging or inhibit growth and learning. Effective facilitators always approach activities with intention, thoughtfulness, and flexibility—evaluating their group and refining their plan as needed.

Many times, I have carefully planned out activities in advance and prepared supplies for a group, only to completely let go of that plan after the group showed it had very different needs from what I expected. In classroom situations, I can carefully plan out a community building curriculum sequence for a specific grade level and, inevitably, find that each class section approaches the activities in a different way. Classes sometimes take a longer or shorter time with an activity than their peers, depending on their strengths, needs, and issues as a group. Individual classes vary in their response to activities as well, gleaning different insights and lessons from the experience. That is the beauty of what we do in experiential facilitation. We meet people where they are and nurture spontaneity of experience to take advantage of teachable moments.

A number of years ago, I designed and implemented an experiential-based, character education curriculum for three 5th grade classrooms in a Wisconsin elementary school. I carefully planned a sequential curriculum to implement, assuming I would use the same lesson plan or set of activities for each of the three classes. As with all groups, however, these 5th grade groups had different group personalities, and although the focus and content areas

of the curriculum remained the same, different lessons emerged for each group during the activities and through processing.

One particular example of a day like this involved an initiative problem I presented to each class. The initiative challenged group members with the task of filling an empty crate in the center of the classroom with an assortment of balls and other throwable objects without stepping into a perimeter area of about 15 feet around the crate. Each of three classes approached this task so  differently, but each had such perfect outcomes for their group's personalities; it always brings a smile when I think of it.

The first group had great difficulty strategizing with each other. This class was socially fragmented by cliques. They often blamed each other. Everyone wanted to do it their own way and have their own turn rather than look at the group goal. It took this group two class sessions to solve the problem, and our processing focused on co-operation, sharing, roles, and group goals versus personal goals.

The second group flew through the problem-solving phase of this task, but had great difficulty keeping each other safe. They came up with the ingenious solution of throwing tennis balls at the crate, forcing it out of the perimeter, and then filling it with the objects. Initially, however, they just couldn't manage to coordinate a way to keep everyone safe from the flying tennis balls. The teacher and I ended up taking advantage of this teachable moment by stopping the group, giving them kudos for their problem-solving skills, and instigating reflection around how they could apply these skills to tak-ing responsibility for others and communicating about group safety.

The third group completed the task in about one third of the time it took the first group. They immediately devised a strategy that involved synergistically working together to pass the balls to those who had proven they had great aim. The others selflessly and steadily worked at retrieving balls and passing them along to the throwers. During reflection the group celebrated the excellent cooperation, communication, and sharing they demonstrated in this activity and how great it felt to operate that way. They discussed how the skills they used so successfully in the game could help them in the group science project they were working on that semester. They were able to identify specific actions that they could take to better approach the school project.

The time of day influenced the facilitation process throughout my time with this school and others. It was evident that the class sessions at the end of the day were the most difficult to facilitate. Students had difficulty remaining focused and on task. With this in mind, the teachers and I rotated the time slots so the different groups would experience these activity sessions at a different time of day each week. This conscious decision to plan around time of day proved successful and continues to influence my work with school groups. Keep in mind that adults also experience fluctuations of energy and engagement (especially around lunch time).

Sequencing Suggestions

- Be ready with a continuum of activities. As a facilitator it is important to have a repertoire of activities that build upon each other. Having activities in your "back pocket" allows you to be ready to deal with changes in direction and learning opportunities that arise in an ever-changing group.

- Be flexible enough to throw out or let go of that well-developed plan if group needs are different from what you expected. Be willing to let go of your agenda to meet the needs of the group.

- "Indicator" activities are helpful. Know some activities that help you read and evaluate the group. For example, before going to the challenge course and teaching safety systems, I facilitate a fun partnered tag activity that involves moving around in a small space and using appropriate touch. This introduces the idea of appropriate touch and close personal space important to the spotting techniques necessary on the challenge course. It also helps me evaluate whether the group is engaged and ready to take the responsibility of balancing fun with safe, focused behavior.

- Pre-group communication is imperative. Take the time to talk with a group's program leader or previous facilitator about the group and its goals, expectations, and personalities. Keep in mind that you will always have to balance that information with your own perceptions and experience of the group.

- Informed consent is critical. Let a group know what they are in for. Informing the group about the upcoming activities doesn't mean giving away the novelty of your approach. Think about informed consent as empowering participants with needed information. For some settings, informed consent is a responsibility of the facilitator in liability situations.

- Continually observe your group and revaluate your plan.

- Be sensitive to the time of day and physical environment when presenting activities.

- Take time to build relationships and trust between group members.

- Be prepared for the unexpected.

- Take advantage of teachable moments.

Knowing Your Group

In order to effectively plan a sequence of meaningful and relevant activities, facilitators need to know basic information about their groups. Answering the following questions can help facilitators design a good program:

- Who is the group and why are they engaging in this program or activity?

- What is their purpose?

- Are there pre-existent individual needs that need to be taken into consideration?

This might seem obvious, but I have found that more often than one would think, busy programs and facilitators miss addressing some of these questions and end up playing catch-up during program time, sometimes with less-than-desirable outcomes. Some facilitators have the opportunity to work with the same groups repeatedly; however, many facilitators work with new groups daily or weekly, with little background knowledge about the group. Regardless of your circumstances, knowing your group is imperative.

In a conversation a few years ago with Gretchen Newhouse, Ph.D., of the Recreation Management/Therapeutic Recreation Department of the University of Wisconsin–LaCrosse, we discussed this

common issue that arises in challenge course programming. We both had found the facilitators we were training and programs we worked with weren't always gathering all of the information they needed prior to the program. We decided to work together to come up with a list of questions to share with our fellow facilitators through the Association of Challenge Course Technology (ACCT) Newsletter (Spring, 2002). Pam McPhee of the University of New Hampshire Browne Center for Innovative Learning shared her program's system for gathering information, including the form her staff sends to every client prior to a group experience.

You might find this checklist valuable when planning your program, whether it involves a challenge course or not. The first step to knowing your group is communication with the group representative. By asking good questions, you receive information that will enable you to successfully prepare for your group. The answers to these questions can provide a guide for your preparation. By asking these same questions of other therapists, counselors, and teachers during common planning time, a one-day program can be adapted to the longer-term setting.

1. **What is the background of the group?** What are the demographics (age, gender, ethnicity, geographic location, etc.)? If you will be facilitating a group with a different background or culture than your own, do some research. Seek insight and understanding by talking with others from that same background/culture. Keep in mind cultural differences in language or slang: Be sensitive to the fact that some words/names we commonly use could be offensive or hurtful.

2. **Does your group know each other?** How well does the group know each other? How long has it been together? What type of setting or work situation is it used to?

   For example, if group members have worked closely together on a project for the last five years, you can probably assume that they have some skills working as a team.

Instead of planning numerous initiatives, low-level, or name game types of activities, prepare for a higher level of activities earlier.

3. **In what experiential education activities has the group participated?** Knowing exactly what activities the group has participated in is essential. As a facilitator, you do want to provide the group with new challenges that are different from the previous activities it has experienced.

   For example, knowing that the group has participated in an activity such as "Name Toss" numerous times with other facilitators allows you to prepare another name game activity for the group. If the group has previously participated in activities with your program or organization, contact previous facilitators for more information. Ask group members which activities they did or did not enjoy.

   Intentionally repeat an activity that the group thoroughly enjoyed. The activity will instantly bring back memories of the fun previously experienced.

4. **What does the group really want to accomplish?** Does the group want to focus on a specific topic or issue? Does the group simply want to have fun? Knowing what the group representative wants the group to accomplish is part of the puzzle. This information can be utilized at the beginning of working with a group. By presenting the goal or desire of the group representative at the beginning, individuals understand the purpose. By receiving group confirmation on the goal, you also will be given its commitment and understanding. The group representative may say the group needs to work on self-esteem; however, many of the group members may feel the true goal is communication. Then discussion of the goal agreed upon by the entire group will guarantee a commitment.

5. **What is the skill level of the group?** Are individuals of varying skill levels? Has the group worked on specific skills

These questions provide a great resource for preparation; however, once the group arrives you will need to be flexible and adjust your facilitation plan based on the changing needs of the group.

before? Was there success? What obstacles were there?

For instance, the group may have worked closely together for 10 years, but the communication between several individuals may have broken down.

6. **What information was given to the participants?** Were the participants given detailed, written information or vague information about the activities? Adjust your introduction to the group based on the feedback. When group members arrive, ask them for information. If they were told nothing about the day, then explain exactly what the activities are all about. Give them the opportunity to ask questions for clarification.

7. **Do the clients know what services/programs you do and don't offer?** Make sure you communicate with the group leader about his or her expectations as a consumer of your program. Be clear about communicating the program's philosophy and methods, as you might find yourself with a group expecting you to provide something you don't feel comfortable providing or are not equipped to deliver.

8. **Are there any problems or issues within the group?** Seek true understanding of the group. Do any underlying problems or issues exist? Are there any problems or issues pending? Are there any past problems or issues? For example, if you receive information that two children constantly fight, you may want to distance these individuals throughout many of the activities.

9. **Do any medical conditions or disabilities exist?** Are there any known medical conditions past or present? Knowing this will provide integral information for planning activities in which the entire group can participate.

Knowing as much as you can about a group before you work with it will increase positive outcomes. The answers to these questions will provide a framework for facilitator preparation. You may want to include additional questions based on your facilitation style or program.

In treatment settings and schools, information about participants is passed on through charting documentation, from counselor to counselor, and/or teacher to teacher. Many facilitators find they have to balance subjective information about groups or students with their own evaluation and experience of the group. In programs where outside groups come to a site, the facilitator needs to gather information from a contact person.

Gretchen and I have both found success in our challenge course programs when sending out a questionnaire for the group leader a few weeks prior to the challenge course experience, and then following it up with a phone call a few days prior to the group session. An example of a form we have used follows. This form is based on a similar form used by Pam McPhee at the University of New Hampshire Browne Center Challenge Course Program in Durham, NH. I have adopted a version of this form for use with our direct service programming, and we have found it useful both for program facilitators and clients.

Program Information

The more we know about your group, the better equipped we will be to design a program and choose activities that address your group's purposes for participating. Please be specific when filling out this form. Feel free to use the reverse side if more space is needed.

Contact Person: _____

Group Name: _____

Number of Participants: _____ Program Date:_____

Background: Tell us about the nature of your group. How long has the group been together? What dynamics exist within the group that may have an impact on its experience?

Prior Experience: Describe any team building or experiential activities this group may have done prior to this workshop.

Goals: What do you wish to accomplish with your group via an adventure experience? These might include: communication, team building, empowerment, problem-solving.

Special Requests: Explain any special requests or needs your group may have.

Next Steps: How does your organization plan to follow up on this experience?

Used with permission from the University of New Hampshire Browne Center for Innovative Learning.

Chapter 3

Creating Ownership &
Facilitating Involvement

Giving Learners Control and Responsibility for Learning

Empowering participants to feel like they own their learning experience and have control from the start of their group experience can encourage participation and "buy-in" by group members. Simple but intentional actions on the part of the facilitator can establish a positive, trusting environment in which participants feel empowered by participation rather than at the mercy of the facilitator.

Think about creating opportunities that build this sense of choice and control for participants from the very beginning of the program. In warm-up activities where someone is in the spotlight (or the middle), make sure there is a rule that allows a person who may be inhibited about being in this position an easy out or an option to participate at their own pace.

For example, when facilitating the well-known icebreaker "Have You Ever?" (Rohnke, 1991), I create an option. This icebreaker calls for a participant to stand in the center of a circle of group members and ask a "have you ever" question. The question involves something he/she has done in order to establish commonalities with fellow group members—for example, "Have you flown a kite?" At that point, everyone in the circle who has flown a kite must leave his/her spot and find a new one, and the person from the center grabs one of those empty spots, leaving someone new in the center to ask a question. The option would be to establish at the beginning of the game an easy buzzword that the person in the center can say if he/she can't think of a "have you ever?" question. My colleague, Michelle Cummings, has another variation that does not use a middle spot at all; instead she uses a different colored spot that is actually part of the perimeter of the Have You Ever? circle. This becomes the question spot. By making it part of the circle, the fun and challenge are maintained while the tension of being the center of attention is reduced.

Creating situations that allow more introverted group members some kind of out or aid gives them an opportunity to participate fully and warm up to group process, trusting that you won't put them in a situation that is embarrassing or puts them on the spot before they are ready. This technique used during a silly warm-up game can pay off later in the group process. By building trust in this way, group members build comfort within the group and are more willing to push their comfort zones later in the group process when it really matters. If some people are challenged too early in a program before any trust builders or warm-ups, a facilitator risks losing them!

Some strategies that I have found to help participants feel what John Dewey called "perceived internal freedom" and in control of their learning include

- Allowing participants to pass in a group discussion, especially at the start of group process.

- Thoughtfully sequencing activities and discussion methods to build comfort within the group incrementally.

- Taking time to get the group warmed up! Start with partner sharing before large group sharing.

- Not calling on people to share in a group, instead creating opportunities for participants to volunteer.

"A master can
tell you what is
expected of you. A
teacher, though,
awakens your own
expectations."
Patricia Neal

Challenge and Choice

The term "challenge by choice"* was coined by Project Adventure,
a leader in the development of experiential-based challenge course
programming. This concept is used to describe the idea that
people should feel that they have control of their adventure experience (Schoel, Prouty, & Radcliffe, 1989; Rohnke & Butler, 1995).
This idea, commonly used in the adventure education setting, can
inform many different types of group work.

I personally like to think of this concept as "challenge AND choice,"
helping to emphasize the concept of personal choice and control.
This concept helps groups recognize that each participant varies
in past experiences, strengths, physical ability, and even emotional
state the day of the activity. Variety in personalities, perspectives,
and experience makes an interesting group. Experiential activities
can be very powerful; any activity that has great power to create
positive change also has the potential to impact someone in a negative way. An activity that might not be intimidating to one person
could paralyze another with fear. The positive outcomes of these

---

* Copyrighted by Project Adventure and used here with permission.

powerful activities can depend on thoughtful facilitation and the participant's perceived control and choice in the situation. Facilitators give learners a sense of power through challenge by choice.

Once in a while, I hear teachers and clinicians say, "But if I give them a choice they won't participate." In response, I go back to the core principles of experiential education and brain-based learning to emphasize the importance of learners' having freedom and choice in their experiences. When John Dewey put forward his ideas about the philosophy of experiential education, he emphasized that participant control is central to learning. I can empathize with these concerned educators who so want their participants to experience the benefits of this kind of group work, but coercion does not work. Setting up parameters for participation does!

A client in a treatment program, a corporate employee, or a student in a classroom is in a somewhat captive or forced situation. They need to participate if they want to receive treatment, keep their job, or get credit for class. Acknowledging this "captive situation" is important. Follow this acknowledgement with realistic parameters for participation. The challenge by choice agreement creates an environment where group participants feel comfortable about setting realistic parameters about how they want to participate. **It is not a choice not to participate, but rather a definition of how one participates in the group activities.**

"Challenge and choice" helps participants understand and define their role in a group more clearly, actually helping them to commit more readily to participation. Group members can take on many different kinds of roles. In school settings, if I have students who are reluctant to participate at first, I arrange with teachers to allow them to sit

on the sidelines and observe. This does not mean they can disrupt or converse with another student who is participating in the activity. Once they are given the freedom to observe for a while, 90% of the time they will find themselves wanting to join the group. However, if I had engaged in a power struggle with them to participate, I might have lost them completely.

If some one chooses not to participate in a specific activity, that does not mean he/she must leave the group. Give these group members an important alternative role, such as encouraging their peers, helping run safety systems, photographing the experience, being a scorekeeper, or aiding the facilitator with equipment. Effective facilitators encourage participants to push their comfort zones and take advantage of opportunities offered. But they also allow participants to set goals and limits for themselves with support from the group, rather than being forced by the group to attempt something that could be a physically or emotionally negative experience.

What Builds Trust?

- "Getting to know you" or icebreaker activities are a key ingredient in trust building. When people form a bond and recognize commonalities, they will be more likely to appreciate differences and demonstrate empathy for each other.

- Give participants an opportunity to build trust in incremental ways by sharing ideas as well as physical trust activities. Give

"Trust people as if they were what they ought to be and you can help them to become what they are capable of being."
Johann Wolfgang von Goethe

participants opportunities to be responsible for each other, show trustworthy behaviors, and demonstrate their investment in the group's success.

- Create situations where it is safe and appropriate for people to ask for and receive help from each other.

- Have group members define trust and trustworthy behaviors and discuss how they perceive and demonstrate those behaviors in particular group situations.

- Teach healthy genuine trust, not contrived coercive behavior. Pushing people into trust situations (such as trust falls from a height) too early in a program or inappropriately with a group can undermine the educational experience.

- Create an environment where group members feel responsible for each other and are willing to speak up when there is a breakdown in communication or an issue that affects the safety or potential experience of the group. It is ideal when the group takes that responsibility rather than the facilitator.

Involving Reluctant Group Members

- Develop an intrinsic motivation for group members to buy into. Some people will jump at the opportunity to help set up equipment or be involved in some other supportive role such as group photographer.

- Focus on positive participation. Give those who are opting out the opportunity to participate passively if they need to for a while (that does not mean distracting the group). Once you draw a critical mass into the group activities, more will follow.

• A successful facilitator has flexible expectations. Remember that sometimes it is appropriate to acknowledge the need for taking "baby steps." Group work is a process, not an event. It is a practice. Learning to play and be part of a group often takes practice for people of all ages. In working with kids, I have discovered that some kids actually never learned how to play, and that many students and adults are not used to working in groups at all.

• Recognize that people learn and are more comfortable interacting in different ways. There are many learning style models and theories that espouse that each of us has a preferred method of learning and interacting with others. Some of us learn better when we can visually see material, others when we are kinesthetically involved in learning. Regardless of the theory you might espouse, it is helpful to differentiate the way you present material and engage group members. Activities that emphasize different skill sets will reach more group members.

• Keep it interesting: Props, humor, and relating activities to popular culture are successful strategies for increasing involvement (see chapter 5).

• Use peers as role models and leaders where appropriate.

Many times participants who were initially hesitant, resistant, or "too cool for school" eventually become the star of the show. Over and over, I see students or staff members who did not engage in class or perform well in previous group situations excel in experientially based group work. This is especially evident when they feel empowered by having choices about their participation and are motivated by intriguing challenges.

In my work with the aforementioned school district, there were many non-participators at first. I decided with the teachers that students could sit out of the activity as long as they were passively involved by watching—not by chatting with a peer. We found that giving them this control and choice empowered them to eventually join in despite themselves! It seemed that it was harder to sit and watch peers enjoy an engaging activity than to join in.

Some of these students were attracted by the offer of helping me with equipment, or by the possibility of being "judge" during a game. Some of the students who were initially the most reluctant and resistant are now the students volunteering to facilitate in extracurricular programs with younger students. I couldn't count the times I have heard teachers/group leaders say something like, "I can't believe how well he participated on the challenge course today; he is never like that in class" or "She never talks in class; I couldn't believe she actually led that activity!" The lasting lesson for facilitators is to find ways to help participants and group leaders transfer these successes back to day-to-day participation in school, work, or other life activities.

Showing Appreciation and Celebrating Success

Include opportunities for celebration. This is a critical part of creating and maintaining a positive environment where participants feel they can take healthy risks, be supported, and leave with some positive growth and success experiences. Unfortunately, in many work and traditional educational settings, time is not regularly

"Celebrate what you want to see more of."
Thomas J. Peters

taken to show appreciation for achievements. People often only get feedback about mistakes or misbehavior.

Your group, therefore, might be awkward with celebrating and giving and receiving feedback. I have worked with many people, especially in school and treatment settings, who seem to have a difficult time giving and receiving compliments and naming their own strengths and positive achievements. They don't seem to get much practice articulating their thoughts, feelings, and reactions, much less giving and receiving feedback with their peers.

Facilitators can help create an atmosphere where group members become comfortable showing appreciation for each other and celebrating success by role modeling a generous spirit toward self

and others and intentionally weaving in celebratory gestures and activities from the very beginning of a group's time together. During introductory activities, encourage group members to give each other a hand or high five. Your excitement and attitude can be contagious, so during competitive icebreakers show appreciation and support toward all of the participants. As the group progresses, celebrating success will become automatic, and they will intuitively make an effort to show sincere appreciation when their peers move outside of their comfort zones. These celebrations create a very empowering atmosphere for group members. The practice of acknowledging and celebrating success and positive moments will likely transfer back to the classroom, workplace, or family.

Compliments

I regularly use this activity with long-term groups to engage participants in giving compliments and feedback in a fun, non-threatening way. This works well with those who know each other well and need some self-esteem boosters and opportunities to celebrate the strengths of group members. A colleague of mine calls it "backstrokes" as people receive compliments and positive feedback, i.e., positive strokes.

Facilitation Suggestions:

- Tape a blank piece of paper on the back of each participant (asking permission first, of course), and give everyone a thin washable marker.

- Instruct group members to visit everyone in the group and write a thoughtful compliment or positive feedback on his or her piece of paper. Explain that they are to focus on personality strengths or positive actions rather than physical characteristics. With school-aged groups, you may need to give clear examples of what kind of compliments are appropriate. For example, "I appreciate your willingness to speak out when you have concern," or "You are very observant," or "You make a great leader."

- After everyone has visited everyone else and written their compliments, give group members the opportunity to sit down and read through their lists.

- Have participants form a circle and share at least one compliment they received on their list.

With clear directions and parameters set at the start, most groups will readily engage and participate in a positive way. This has been especially effective with adolescents who may lack self-esteem and don't give and receive positives very often.

Establishing or Formalizing Group Norms

Group norms are the values and characteristics that exist in every a group. They include code of conduct, acceptable behaviors or customs, habits, and expectations about how things will be done. Group norms influence how group members communicate and work together. Norms can hinder or help a group in the process of achieving its goals. Often members aren't aware of some of the group norms that they have created. Creating a formal time and space to explore existing group norms for behavior and language is part of giving the group control over its learning experience.

Many people live day to day in an atmosphere where little thought is given to the power of language. When a group intentionally works together to agree on clarifying and establishing norms that all members can endorse, the group becomes stronger, more effective, and more aware of its dynamics and behavior. The process of establishing the norms can become a team building activity in itself. When facilitating this process remember that these norms will change and need to be clarified throughout the group process.

As mentioned previously, it is reasonable and important for the facilitator to set basic ground rules and expectations when first interacting with a group. There is an important difference between program- and facilitator-driven ground rules or expectations and the group norms or values agreements created by the entire group. It is after the group has experienced some time working together,

---

* A description of "The Full Value Contract" is found in *Islands of Healing*, copyright 1986, Project Adventure.

seeing its strengths and weaknesses and actually experiencing some conflict or struggle together, that creating and clarifying its own norms will become especially relevant, valuable, and necessary.

The time spent up front and throughout a program focusing on establishing and reflecting on positive group norms is time well spent, maximizing outcomes for the group and individuals. Helping the group create behavioral norms regarding comments and judgments during group activities and discussions increases the amount of sharing and interaction and enhances the depth of group experience. Many facilitators guide their group to create agreements of some kind.

Project Adventure, one of the first organizations to specialize in providing challenge course curriculum for schools, has developed a concept for this idea: The Full Value Contract*. In another exploration of the moral dimensions of the classroom, teacher and author Vivian Paley (1992) describes in her book *You Can't Say You Can't Play* how she came to the conclusion that something had to be done in her classroom to create an environment of acceptance and care. After 25 years of teaching, she decided she had seen and heard enough students hurt each others' feelings through exclusion

during playtime. In her engaging writing style, Paley describes the process of implementing the "you can't say you can't play" idea in her classroom with her students' involvement and input throughout the process. She

"Coming together is a beginning; keeping together is progress; working together is success." Henry Ford

shares the ensuing changes that took place in her classroom and school as a result of the co-creative norms agreement she implemented with her students (Paley, 1992).

As mentioned previously, new research in the neuroscience field about the brain and learning demonstrates that a positive learning environment can have a positive impact on learning (Jensen, 1998). The development of brain-based learning theory reinforces the idea that groups will benefit when facilitators intentionally guide group participants to consciously create this kind of positive learning environment within their group (Jensen, 2000). When asked to reflect on this idea, most people of all ages agree that when they do not feel safe and supported or are undervalued or put down by their peers, they do not succeed as readily as they would in a more supportive environment. Though many know this to be true, they have not spent time conceptualizing this idea.

The idea of establishing positive norms in a group setting makes common sense to most of us. Many people attribute bullying and harassment behaviors in schools and workplaces to the lack of attention to establishing prosocial group norms. Why is a formal process of creating positive group norms not undertaken more often in group situations? In working with teachers and facilitators, I have found that most people agree that the concept of formalizing positive group norms is a good one, but they often find it difficult

to facilitate with their group. Or they help a group create an agreement early on in group process but find that they don't effectively reinforce and follow up on the agreements as the group continues.

In contemplating why facilitators and groups sometimes struggle with formalizing positive group norms, I have observed that one possibility is that facilitators try to process a group norms agreement too early in the group's experience. The first meeting, first day, or first hour (depending on the length of time the group will meet) is not likely to be an appropriate time to create meaningful or relevant agreements. This is a common pitfall. When this activity is attempted before a group has time to learn about each other and develop its group personality, taking into consideration strengths and weaknesses, there really aren't any norms to address.

After the group has experienced some activities together, this process becomes more authentic. For shorter (one-day) programs the process of establishing group norms might be more streamlined and a brief, less involved process, but would still be most effectively placed after the group has had some time together. It could be revisited throughout the day and become part of the group closing or even something the participants take with them from the program.

For longer-term programs this process is most effective when developed with the group over time. Combined with reflective practice and regular feedback and evaluation, it becomes a meaningful and useful tool for the group. Facilitators are often stymied by the idea of a boring contract or list of rules. This barrier is lifted when one thinks of this activity not as "housekeeping," but as an interesting and engaging activity that can involve different mediums. By presenting the group norms agreement task in different ways—combining list making, artwork, using props, and discussion—it becomes a richer, more significant, and memorable experience.

Establishing an agreement focused on valuing group members is not a rule that should be mandated, but more of a concept to be introduced to a group to think about, develop, and make its own.

It is practice. Remember that this is often a new concept, and new skills take practice. Facilitators report getting discouraged when a group doesn't stick to its agreement. Measure its success as a practice. **This is a process, not an event.**

Helping participants create a "standard of care" in the group atmosphere can be one of the areas teachers and facilitators find most difficult; however, it can be incredibly rewarding for everyone involved. When participants are given the opportunity to take part in this process, most choose to adopt it and take it very seriously. It helps group members understand the power of language, both positive and negative. Many practitioners and group members have observed that this concept, presented in the educational setting on the challenge course, often permeates into other areas of life.

The idea of valuing the experience does not require that participants be best friends with everyone in their classroom, work group, or program. Ideally, group members come to recognize that they and their peers have value and can offer important contributions to the group experience. If students appreciate the experience and value the group (both others and themselves), they end up with a more "valuable" outcome. A facilitator can help a group define norms in many ways. I usually start this ongoing group process with simple list making and discussion. As the group develops, artwork and symbols become effective. A great start to the process is a simple list defining what is "Us" and "Not Us."

Participant-Directed Group Norms Agreements

Us/Not Us List

The Us/Not Us List is a quick method I learned from my colleagues Jim Grout and Nicki Hall at High 5 Adventure Learning Center to help group members begin the process of evaluating, looking at, and thinking about their behavior. I see it as a first step for creating group norms that will be followed up and built upon later. This activity highlights key issues and concerns such as the power of language and behavior in group process. This first step should happen near the initial stages of group formation but after the group is warmed up.

Facilitation Suggestions:

- Take a large piece of paper, and divide it into two columns: "Us" and "Not Us."

- List the characteristics group members want to have in their group under "Us."

- List the characteristics group members want to keep out of their group under "Not Us."

Outcomes/Processing Ideas:

- Often when involving group members in this initial activity, I ask whether they plan to have sarcasm on the Us or Not Us side. It always leads to an interesting conversation. Often group members doesn't come to a conclusive decision about it at this stage, but the very fact that they start talking and sharing about the issue seems to make them more aware of the power of their words.

- This can be a great opportunity to talk about showing appreciation for group and individual success. Have members talk about how they can demonstrate positive appreciation.

- Focusing on the positive truly does lead to positive change. I have found that as the group develops, the need for the "Not Us" part of the list falls away if there is enough focus on the "Us" side. Letting go of the negative allows the positive to shine through.

- Often groups just need more information about and practice with using positive language and opportunities to practice positive behavior. In school and treatment settings, kids are bombarded with information about what they shouldn't do. It is nice to explore what they can do for a change.

- Regardless of the method used, the group norms agreement is most useful when it is placed where the group has access to it and can refer to it and refine it during the time it works together.

Us/Not Us Sample List

Us	Not Us
Responsible	Whiners
Community	Too serious
Persevere	Controlling
Agree to disagree	Gossip
Empathetic	Careless
Honoring gifts	Alienating/excluding
Kind	Territorial
Tolerant	Rigid
Open	Not trusting
Resilient	Competitive for resources
Consistent	Resentful
Light-hearted	Violent
Diversity	Sarcastic
Share	Fearful
Honor differences	Angry
Loyal	Judgmental
Give 100%	Critical
Take care of self	
Practice mindfulness	
Supportive	
Positive	
Flexible	
Trusting	
Cooperative	
Compassionate	
Respectful	
Intentional	

Group Symbols

As groups progress through development, it can be effective to revisit group norms in a different way. Giving the group an opportunity to create or find a symbol for its strengths and goals is one way to facilitate this process. You can present reflective tools—such as postcards, objects, puzzle pieces, or Chiji Cards*— that involve symbols of the groups experiences or successes as it progress through activities. Often groups will latch onto a symbol that can later be part of its "group norms symbol."

For example, one particular adventure facilitation workshop group found that the turtle Chiji card represented its early group experiences together. When it came time to create a formal values agreement, the group chose to draw an outline of 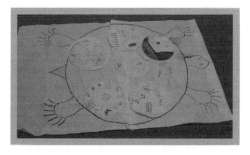 a turtle. Group members then filled it in with drawings and words describing the strengths they each brought to the group, their commitment to the group, and the goals the group had defined for itself. They felt the turtle represented moving forward with these ideas in a slow and steady way. The group carried the symbol with it throughout the program and took a group picture with it at closing. These group members still refers to themselves as "the turtles" when they communicate with me.

Many facilitators share their success in using figural representations of group experience. A well-known activity in the adventure education field is "The Being" by Boys Harbor in Long Island, which involves a drawn outline of a group member filled with the

---

* Chiji Cards are a processing tool created by Steve Simpson, Buzz Bocher, and Dan Miller, founders of the Institute for Experiential Education. Chiji is a Chinese word meaning important moment or opportunity. See resources.

group's commitments. Outside the figure are the things the group members want to "leave out" of their group.

With another group we created a "being" drawing as described above, but took a second step when we revisited our group norms after a series of sessions together. In that reflection session the group ceremoniously cut away the negative behaviors the group had wanted to keep out, in order to demonstrate that with time and practice we had been successful in focusing on the positive group behaviors, allowing the negatives to fall away.

Recently, I had success turning this into an "action figure," symbolizing a group's commitment to acting in certain ways. The group members wrote things they wanted to say or that should be talked about near the mouth. They wrote the kinds of things they would like to hear from others by the ears, what they hoped to feel and own by the heart, etc. There was no naming of the negative at this point, just positive actions.

Another variation of using art to represent an agreement was created by Jeanella Bentley, a teacher in Bridgeport, Connecticut. She had students create a drawing of their school. Inside the school, they wrote and drew what they thought should be part of their group experience. Outside the school they drew a dumpster filled with the negative behaviors they wanted to keep out.

Jigsaw Puzzles

Using tangible objects to represent individual and group values agreements can be a powerful method for involving groups in interesting group norms discussions and creating a lasting representation of the group's goals and commitments. Creative facilitators use group  sculptures, structures, towers, and other tangible group creations to represent the individual efforts that make a group successful.

One of my favorite methods to reinforce the idea of individual responsibility and its relationship to the group uses a jigsaw puzzle. The puzzle pieces can represent the individuals' roles, strengths, or commitments to the group and how they relate to the whole.

Adventure educators have used giant jigsaw puzzles as a team building initiative for years. I used one that was part of the school's game bag to help students articulate the positive components they thought were necessary in a group. I attached paper to each puzzle piece and had students write a positive group norm on their puzzle piece and then put the puzzle together as a group. This method helped them better express themselves as it was easier for them to share their perspectives when attaching them to an object. During a conflict situation, they were able to use the puzzle pieces to name their part in the conflict and the "piece" they might take on to change it.

When putting together a program for a group of school administrators who were striving to define their roles, I cut cork board into pieces and asked group members to decorate their pieces in a way that defined their role and commitment to the group. They ended up taking the pieces home and decorating them in very individualistic ways that represented how they viewed their own "piece of the puzzle." One group member cut her puzzle piece into five pieces that represented the many different aspects of her role in the group. Another participant just glued a giant pair of sunglasses to her piece as she felt it represented the "big picture" role she needed to take in the group. It ended up leading to an incredibly powerful discussion about each group member's strengths, fears, hopes, and level of commitment to the group. They kept it for a reference as they worked together throughout the year.

You can make your own giant puzzle if you have a jigsaw handy. I like to use blank puzzle pieces made by The Community Puzzle™. They offer interchangeable pieces sold in bulk that can be combined to create very large puzzles for many group members. They are available at www.communitypuzzle.com.

Group Norms Example

During graduate school I worked with a women's hockey team. The team was experiencing a losing season, and the coach and captains felt a formal team building experience might help them learn more about improving their performance. After meeting with the coach and captains, I set up a series of afternoon sessions using community building activities, followed with a day on the challenge course. As part of the process team members kept journals or reflection papers that the coach asked them to share with me.

To be honest, at that time in my work I was in the habit of breezing through the group norms process with most groups. I usually just presented a full-value agreement idea at the start of a program from a very facilitator-driven approach: laying out ground rules for participation and trying to get them to think about "valuing" each other fully. I led group members in a discussion, asking them questions like: What does the word "value" mean? What does valuing yourself, others, and the group experience mean? How do you think you could make this the most "valuable" experience possible? I then asked them to quickly brainstorm ways they show they value themselves, each other, and the experience. Although I think it was useful to plant this seed with groups to get them thinking about their values and behavior, I was missing out on important learning opportunities that arise when participants spend more time on exploring group norms together as a group.

This became very clear to me during my team building experience with the women's hockey team. Thinking that I wouldn't need to spend a great deal of time on group norms, I got right into facilitating problem-solving activities with the group. The women were pretty enthusiastic with the group icebreakers and problem-solving. They were obviously a talented and capable group of women.

As we got into more activities it became apparent that there was a great deal of tension among team members. I started hearing sarcastic comments, and, as we got into a particularly challenging activity, the frustration came to a head with blaming and accusations, splitting the group. When I read the reflection papers from the team members following that session, there were many comments about the persistent negative atmosphere on the team and how that day's events truly represented what was happening with the team on the ice. Excerpts from these entries follow:

"When the pursuit of natural harmony is a shared journey, great heights can be attained."
Lynn Hill

"We need to build a culture of respect. We have a problem with negative comments, talking behind each other's back, and blaming others for our failures."

"The blaming and the bad-mouthing must stop."

"Our biggest problem is communication and HOW we communicate with each other when we are frustrated. We make jokes instead of talking about the issue. We complain about each other behind each other's back. We make sarcastic comments instead of saying what we really feel."

"At one point when we were able to put the blaming aside and stay positive with our communication we were successful—we need to figure out how to do this all of the time on the ice."

I realized how important a group norms discussion could be for this group. We used the next session to create a formal group norms agreement together. This led us to having a very extensive discussion about their language and the use of sarcasm, taking up the larger part of that afternoon's session. It was a turning point for the group. We continued on to successfully participate in another afternoon session and a challenge course day.

In the feedback papers after the program ended, the hockey players mentioned repeatedly that the group norms discussions about language and the activities we had participated in around that subject had been the most important part of the program.

"Though I really enjoyed the challenge course activities—challenging myself and trying new things—it was that afternoon we spent in the locker room hashing through our communication issues that was the most important moment for me."

"The full-value agreement was the best part of this training; the process of brainstorming what is okay and not okay behavior for members of this team really made us think about our back-stabbing and negative comments and how they were paralyzing us as a team."

"I think the most difficult activity we did was when we had to get in a circle around a hula hoop and bring it to the ground equally. It was a lot harder than we expected and everyone started blaming everyone else for which side of the hoop was too high or too low.

That got everyone frustrated and made it impossible. After we took a break and got positive with our communication it was no problem."

"I wasn't too excited about participating in this team building stuff at first—I thought it would be the same old hokey games. But it wasn't; it ended being harder than we thought and this struggle brought us together. Our discussion on sarcasm was the most important part of the training and the piece most of us have taken 'back to the ice.'"

Reading these reflection papers brought home for me how valuable taking the time to work with a group to formalize and discuss norms is to the experiential learning process. Since that time it has become a more regular part of my practice, especially with long-term groups. Their comments inspired me to look at the process as an opportunity to help a group create positive cultural change.

Tap into your and your group's creativity. Norms agreements can take many forms. The most important aspect is the process itself. Group norms discussions can be great opportunities to introduce difficult subjects. I have witnessed many groups engage in difficult discussions about sarcasm in their workplace or on their team with the outcome of important values agreements that changed the way they work together.

People grow and change through conflict and struggling with problems. The value of experiential-based group work is that it enables a group of people to grow from a group into a team. Groups are a collection of people with some common purpose. The formalization of group norms helps groups become well-working teams by establishing behaviors that guide their interactions and help them achieve their goals.

Recognize that it takes time for this process to unfold and that it is not a "one-shot deal." Aim for the group to become aware of its norms regarding values and behaviors and the need to evaluate and readjust them as it grows and changes.

Chapter 4

Aspects of
Effective Facilitation

"The leadership instinct you are born with is the backbone.
You develop the funny bone and the wishbone that go with it."
Elaine Gather

Successful facilitators consciously think about their style and continually develop it through a variety of intentional ways, including
reflection, feedback, continued education, and experimentation.
Integral to the idea of experiential education is the recognition that
learners are individuals with differing needs and preferences as
to how they best learn and retain information, and how they best
interact in groups (this is often referred to as individual learning
style). Successful educators are always reflecting on their own
style and methods. They take into consideration the strengths and
preferences that exist in every group with the intention of meeting
the differing needs of participants. Hopefully it is a dynamic, ever-
changing growth process.

As facilitators mature in their practice, they learn to know their
strengths and capitalize on them. Through reflection they learn
their value as a facilitator and the idea of "going with their gut."
An effective facilitator knows how to set appropriate boundaries
with group members. An ethical facilitator understands his/her
scope of practice and limitations.

Being open to experimentation, learning from others, and trying new ideas and methods are integral to developing effective facilitation skills. This practice helps keep the work of facilitation interesting and fulfilling. "Failing forward"—being able to recognize mistakes and learn from them—makes one adept at handling difficult group situations with confidence and finesse.

Keep learning and reflecting! Effective facilitators make an effort to balance theory and practice. It is important for even the seasoned professional to attend conferences and workshops, read the theoretical foundations of the field, and keep up with research as they practice. Conversely, those who have spent a great deal of time studying theory in the academic world have to put themselves out there to practice facilitation. Facilitation is an art that has to be practiced!

Take a Risk

Put yourself out there to share your experiences with others in your field. Take a risk; try something new. Also trust your instincts about the methods and style that works for you—don't try to be someone else. Build on your strengths, but also be aware that sometimes a strength and a weakness are opposite ends of the same quality! For example, if you are a facilitator who is very comfortable "flying by the seat of your pants" and being spontaneous, it probably is a

"The value of an idea lies in using it."
Thomas Edison

"Progress always involves risk. You can't steal second base and keep your foot on first."
Frederick B. Wilcox

strength in that you are able to be flexible and adapt to the changing needs of the group. Paradoxically there are times when this strength could become a weakness if agenda items don't get met. With this in mind, you can recognize times when making an effort to be more structured or asking for a co-facilitator with that strength could benefit your group. Knowing your strengths and when to outsource or share responsibility for a group with someone else is also a thoughtful, reflective way to approach facilitation. Different styles fit different groups.

Flexibility and willingness to try new things are great qualities in a facilitator. If we don't try new activities and approaches we can become bored with ourselves and our work. Sharing and exploring is one of the fundamental aspects of experiential education. One of the wonderful qualities of the art and science of education is that there is no best way. Good teachers recognize they are learners. There is something to be learned from every group experience.

Welcome the Unexpected

"All life is an experiment." Ralph Waldo Emerson

Try new activities that seem like they might fit your program needs (always keeping in mind the physical and emotional safety of participants). Don't be discouraged if you present an activity that flops. That is how we sometimes learn best! You might benefit from asking the group for ideas about how it could be improved or changed. Who knows, the group members may help you develop a brand new activity or interesting twist. Remember that you can learn a great deal from activities that don't work quite as you planned. Expect every activity to be different with different groups. Make sure to let your participants teach you a few things. I made some valuable discoveries about a tool or technique during situations when the group was a different size from what I expected, when I didn't have the materials I needed, when the group's behavior required an on-the-spot intervention, or when the group's creativity took the activity in an unexpected direction.

One example of this accidental success happened during my graduate school experience at Minnesota State–Mankato, where I was a graduate assistant for MSU's challenge course program. I was facilitating a group of young adolescent boys who were part of a group home. This challenging group attended our program for two days. Day one of the low and high ropes course initiatives was successful. Throughout that first day the group engaged in a variety of reflective techniques including Chiji Cards, in which the participants were presented with a series of pictures and chose the symbol that best represented their feeling, idea, or role in the group.

When the group arrived on day two to participate in rappelling on our climbing tower, conflict was apparent. During some warm-up activities, they were not focused, made derogatory comments to each other, and exhibited behaviors that were not conducive to participating in the rappel tower. It seemed like we had taken several steps backward from the day before. I had to make a decision about my role as a facilitator that would affect the rest of the day.

I stopped the activity we were doing and asked the group to sit under a tree. I told them that we couldn't go on like this if they wanted to do the rappel tower, and that I was close to calling the bus to pick them up. I asked them to sit together for a while and make a decision about their participation as a group and figure out

"Name the greatest of all inventors: Accident."
Mark Twain

if they could or wanted to change. On a whim, I tossed them the deck of Chiji Cards and said, "Maybe these will help."

About 10 minutes later, the other teachers and I came back to the group. The kids were seated in a circle under the tree; they were focused and attentive to each other. One student spoke for the group and stated that they had chosen the "eagle" card to represent their need to "soar above" their petty squabbling and "soar" on the rappel tower. They seemed sincere about this commitment to "rise above."

The boys were true to their words, and any time a group member demonstrated the slightest negative behavior, a peer would intervene immediately by asking, "Are you soaring?" It turned out to be a wonderfully successful day. The social workers who chaperoned the group were surprised and pleased. It was the first time they had witnessed the student who spoke for the group taking the lead and speaking during group process.

That accidental success with the cards informed future facilitation. I started using Chiji Cards and other participant-centered reflective tools in different ways. Seeing the benefit of the participant-directed approach of these tools, my view of how they could be used was significantly enhanced. I have continued to use the cards in conflict situations with great success. The co-creative process between facilitator and group can be a rewarding synergistic relationship.

Another example of accidental success happened when I was working with the operations staff of a metropolitan opera company on a day of team building. The director had contracted with us for a day to rejuvenate staff, explore communication, and get dialogue going about their systems and how they were functioning as a team.

I presented one of my favorite initiatives called "Fill the Crate" (see the following description). In the past, groups had solved this problem in a variety of ways, from a synergistic method of repeatedly tossing and retrieving, to tying shoes and shirts together to lasso and drag the crate out of the center to fill it, to throwing one of the items at the crate to move it out of the circle.

Usually, I encourage participants to use only what they brought with them. However, I forgot to mention this rule that day. When all of the items ended up inside the perimeter and the group was stuck and frustrated, one of the participants went to the side of the gym and grabbed a giant ladder we used for setting up the challenge course. I normally would not have allow this, but I felt checked about saying anything.

The group pushed the crate out of the center using the ladder and filled it with all of the objects. When it was finished, one of the par-

ticipants said, "We did it, but I am not happy about HOW we did it. It is just like us. We are given a challenge to solve a problem—like putting on an opera production. We don't communicate well, plan ahead, or make the best use of our strengths and resources. At the last minute, we have to call in the "big guns" from outside to fix it. I think we can better utilize our own resources!"

At that point, the group decided to put the ladder back. The participants started the initiative again, made a solid plan, and systematically worked to get the balls in the crate. Some group members were tossers and others were retrievers, using a string of belts to retrieve. The company manager later told me this was a very significant moment for them as a group. I was glad I stepped back and didn't limit their use of that ladder.

Fill the Crate

This is a variation of a game I learned in a workshop given by Jim Schoel of Project Adventure many years ago. It has changed a great deal over time, but was inspired by his original problem.

Equipment:
Milk crate full of throwables of various shapes, sizes, and weight
Large perimeter rope
2nd perimeter rope for a planning circle

Facilitation Suggestions:

- Create a large perimeter circle on the ground with the rope.

- Empty the crate of throwables outside the perimeter.

- Place the empty crate in the middle of the circle.

- Challenge the group to get the throwables into the crate without stepping into the circle, moving the rope, or talking. (Experiment with the no talking rule; younger groups will have a hard time with this. A good option is to create another circle away from the problem where the group is allowed to talk).

Outcomes/Processing Ideas:
This game can lead to great discussions around planning ahead, communication, dealing with frustrations, leadership, and looking at a problem from different perspectives.

Attitude is Everything

"Whether you think you can or think you can't—
you are right." Henry Ford

Group participants truly respond—even subconsciously—to a facilitator's attitudes, demeanor, and expectations. We often communicate more than we realize with our body language and tone. A positive attitude is contagious. If you really believe in the methods and activities you are using with a group, they will most likely buy in and respond to your enthusiasm. Conversely, if you aren't comfortable with the material you are presenting, group members can sense that as well. Participants also respond to your attitudes toward them. I believe if we expect the best of participants, they will usually perform their best.

We all work with difficult groups and group situations at times. Beware of focusing only on the negative behaviors. Remember

"There is a soul force in the universe which, if we permit it, will flow through us and produce miraculous results." Mahatma Gandhi

to acknowledge and believe in the abilities of the learners in your group. If you are starting to feel there is "no hope for that kid" or a participant is "pushing your buttons," then it might be time for some self-reflection. Take a step back and reflect on the positive aspects and achievements that have occurred; recognize the small steps and successes of the individuals and the group. It could be that it is time to get some support and new perspectives from a colleague, or if possible find a co-facilitator for the group.

During a recent conversation with a group of teachers about the challenges of working with middle school students, I said, "When I work with that 7th grade group, I keep thinking of the comedy film *What about Bob?* (1991), where the main character (played by Bill Murray) is guided by his psychiatrist (Richard Dreyfus) to repeat the mantra 'baby steps' as he gets over his phobias. I try to recognize each 'baby step' the group members are taking. If I didn't, I could become very discouraged." One of the teachers responded, "Yes, we have to remind ourselves that we are looking for 'oak kind of growth' rather than expecting 'mushroom kind of growth.'" I have observed that facilitators who regularly work with challenging populations are skilled at acknowledging and celebrating the small successes and adept at noticing the small, positive steps forward a group is making.

"The last human freedom is to choose one's attitude in any given set of circumstances."
Viktor Frankl

One example of how attitudes can affect us is illustrated in an experience an intern and I had with a group of adults from a local company. I was warned by the company contact person that a couple of group members were very resistant about attending and would likely be difficult. This is not unusual with people who are asked to come as part of work; they often feel coerced into coming or intimidated at the idea of participating in interactive activities with their colleagues.

This was one of the first times my intern had facilitated a corporate group. She joined us a little late, so I was not able to brief her on the dynamics of the group. The group did have some difficult moments they worked through, but there was some great dialogue. Although one participant had some difficult behaviors, he stayed with the group, and the other participants never allowed him to negatively affect their process together.

At the end of the day, I felt it had been a success for the group as a whole, although at times it had been challenging. My intern had a different perspective (remember that she had not been warned about the group dynamics). She had focused in on the negative comments of the one participant and was exhausted by his attitude and comments, taking them personally. It struck me how we had ended up with very different perspectives of the day that I believe had more to do with our own attitudes and expectations rather than the group's behaviors.

All of us have times when we question our effectiveness. Group facilitation is not easy. It takes a great deal of energy and commitment, as well as a willingness to take on challenging interpersonal situations. Facilitators who continue to enjoy their work remain hopeful, keep their perspective of the big picture, and recognize that growth and change arise from conflict and struggle. Consistently practicing patience, empathy, and the power of positive thinking reaps great rewards.

Know the Why Behind What You Do

Take time to study the theory behind what you do. Reflect and observe what works in your groups, and consciously develop your own philosophy of facilitation. Reading about theories of experiential education, facilitation, and learning helps refine your practice and develop clear purpose. Engaging in the study of theoretical foundations of experiential education from Greek philosophers to John Dewey during my time in graduate school added a lot of depth to my work. My introduction to Taoist philosophy through my work with Steven Simpson (2003) and his book *The Leader Who is Hardly Known* changed my perspective on my role as a facilitator.

The study of experiential education philosophy combined with systematic research on my own practice of facilitation helped me become clearer about some of the choices I make as a facilitator and why I gravitate toward particular activities and methods. Donald Schon (1983) in his book *The Reflective Practitioner* refers to this as one's "theory in use" or the theories that drive our actions. Our theory in use is the set of concepts we work by, that help us design experiences and explain the why behind what we do. This theory in use helps me target my goals and objectives and be more intentional in my practice of facilitation.

Keep up to date with new trends in the field of education, psychology, brain research, and other related fields. This information will inform and improve your practice, giving new insights into why certain practices work well and why some old practices should be replaced. It can also provide a rationale and validation for experiential methods that help generate buy-in from managers, school administrators, and others who want to know the value of this approach. Being able to articulate why and how experiential methods work makes you more effective and credible as a practitioner.

Some specific trends in education that I have found especially worth paying attention to are brain research, brain-based learning theory, and learning styles theory. Brain-based learning theory promotes problem-based learning and community-building activities as integral tools for brain development. Eric Jensen (2000) in his books *Teaching with the Brain in Mind* (1998) and *Brain Based Learning* shares specific aspects of this research that support the very tenets of experiential education, such as the importance of being actively involved in learning and that reflective practice and the use of symbols and metaphor enhance learning outcomes.

The education field is paying attention to brain research as it demonstrates ways to improve academic outcomes. For me specifically, I have gained new inroads in many educational settings by connecting the brain-based research with experiential methods. It has provided new ideas on how to better meet the needs of participants with whom I am working, increased my awareness of the effect of environment on learning, and confirmed the importance of intentionally using a variety of methods to engage groups in learning.

"Intention is a powerful force. Coming from the Latin word that means 'to stretch toward,' intention is the initial bending of your mind toward a target. It is the force that permeates the journey and the goal. A story from the medieval Christian tradition illustrates intention: A traveler came to a worksite and saw two men carrying stones. One man was working listlessly, with a sullen expression on his face, while the other man was cheerfully singing as he busily carried stone after stone. 'What are you doing?' asked the traveler of the sullen worker. 'Laying stone,' was his reply. 'What are you doing?' the industrious worker was asked. 'Building a cathedral,' was his reply. This is intention at work." The Corporate Mystic: A Guidebook for Visionaries with Their Feet on the Ground by Gay Hendricks and Kate Ludeman

Studying the various learning style theories and models has also helped validate the use of experiential education and make an argument for this approach in the public schools and business world. There is a movement in education to differentiate instruction, i.e., to find ways to vary the delivery of lessons to meet the different learning styles of students or group members. Many traditional educators have found the field of experiential education to be a resource, giving them the tools to do this in their setting. Recently, I was asked to coteach a class on "differentiated instruction" when the curriculum coordinator recognized that the experiential methods we use can help teachers develop practical strategies for varying the delivery of their lessons.

Learning style theories not only help validate experiential facilitation practice, but also inform it. They remind me to balance kinesthetic activities with quiet reflection and dialogue, attempting to meet the varying needs of learners. They inspire me to use learning styles inventories as a group activity to help group members comprehend how their individual strengths and differences affect the way they work together, understand and empathize with those who are different, and find new ways to work and interact with each other. Knowing and being able to articulate the why behind what you say helps create intention and a thoughtful, deliberate, and goal-directed approach to your work.

"In creating, the only hard thing is to begin."
James Russell Lowell

Creativity

Everyone has the ability to be creative, but not everyone recognizes they have it. I have heard many adults and adolescents say "I am not creative." I find that somewhere around adolescence, people who aren't skilled artists start to think they aren't creative. Artistic ability and creativity are not the same thing.

I think most people who are drawn to facilitation are creative. Ask yourself: Have you ever changed your plan midstream because of bad weather, a space issue, or an unexpected number of participants? Have you ever taught a lesson or facilitated an activity without the materials you hoped to use? Have you ever dealt with a difficult situation or behavioral issue in a group? If you answered yes to any of these questions, you should give yourself some credit for using creativity.

Creativity can be defined in many different ways. Some think of it as the ability to bring something new into being, but it is also defined as the ability to use something in a different way or make new associations between existing ideas and concepts.

I believe creative facilitators aren't just those who create new activities, but rather they are those who have the ability to make new associations with existing tools and activities and find new ways to present or use an activity. Creative facilitators are able to take advantage of opportunities that spontaneously arise and make them part of a lesson or activity. They are able to navigate an unexpected change of plan or "make lemonade out of lemons" if a difficult situation arises. They are able to pick up on an idea or new direction mentioned by a participant and make it part of the activity or lesson. It has a lot to do with attitude and perspective and a willingness to take a risk.

Creativity is improved with practice. With experience and an open mind, facilitators become adept at thinking on their feet. They are able to recognize and take advantage of "teachable moments" as they arise. To nurture creativity, facilitators must be willing to go with the flow and take advantage of unplanned opportunities. If your group takes the activity or discussion somewhere unexpected, be flexible enough to go with it if appropriate. There are many examples in this book of favorite facilitation tricks and tools created through positive accidents in facilitation. Being open to these opportunities is one of the qualities that makes for a successful group facilitator.

Nurturing creativity in learners is what experiential education is all about. Teaching creativity and insight is impossible, but giving opportunities for people to learn it for themselves is integral to the art of participant-directed facilitation. A co-creative relationship between the facilitator and group members can take the group's learning further. Be open to what the group members have to teach you; listen to their humor, popular culture references, or references to life situations, and use the information to make the learning more relevant and engaging. Your group might help you discover a whole new way of approaching or engaging in an activity. Spontaneity and variety make working with people more interesting and worthwhile.

Co-Facilitation

Many of us facilitate alone most of the time. The irony in group facilitation is that those of us who take the role of facilitator are generally quite comfortable leading and planning on our own and even prefer it. We develop our own favorite activities, methods, and styles and become comfortable in our role of leader or guide. We often find it difficult to facilitate with others, despite the fact that we are working with teams.

Facilitators can be reticent about sharing creative license, communicating plans, or letting go of controlling the "plan for the day." Those whose work requires that they lead groups with other people often share that co-facilitation is one of the most challenging

"Cooperation is the thorough conviction that nobody can get there unless everybody gets there."
Virginia Burden

aspects of their jobs but also the most beneficial and rewarding. I know there are times when I have dreaded co-facilitating because of a possible difference in style, philosophy, or methods with my co-leader, or simply because it takes time and energy to plan and communicate with someone else rather than keeping it in my own head. But ah..., isn't practicing compromise, communication, and coordination with others usually what we are trying to facilitate with our clients? Sometimes we teach what we most need to know.

Co-facilitating can be most valuable for the reasons I just mentioned. Communication and conflict can bring growth. Having to explain our ideas and plans to someone else helps us reflect on our rationale, which pushes us to look at our strengths and weaknesses while articulating our methods. This begins a co-creative process that can be incredibly rewarding for both facilitators. I've learned most of my favorite activities, methods for introductions, and fun stylistic twists from other facilitators. Taking the time and effort to work out plans and differences in philosophy and approach can be painful, but it definitely has improved my practice.

Our relationships with the people we work with inform our work in group facilitation. The reflection involved in organizing our thoughts and articulating our philosophy, methods, and rationale for activities and approaches, while accepting someone else's, helps us become better facilitators and have more empathy around the process we are often guiding. Having to explain and give reasons for our approaches and receiving feedback from another practitioner on planned activities gives us insight into our practice as a facilitator.

Facilitators who work alone could find creating opportunities for collaborative work beneficial. Those who work alone are often at risk of getting stuck in the rut of relying on only their view of the world. If you are someone who does not have the opportunity to co-lead groups in your daily practice, try to create those opportunities by co-leading a conference presentation in your field or by co-leading an in-service with another staff person.

Participants benefit from the combination of two or more different teaching styles. Facilitators are often more effective as a team. The varying strengths and perspectives that each brings to the field make the experience interesting and rewarding. By opening ourselves to working with others, we are creating a richer experience and in many ways being "truer" to the concept of interactive group work. When we co-facilitate well, we model to the group the value of collaboration and teach effective teamwork by example.

Taking the time to plan together and to check in after a group can help co-leaders work effectively. Journaling and keeping a record of activities helps co-leaders plan, organize, and follow up together. Debriefing afterward, in an atmosphere where we can safely celebrate successes and communicate concerns and frustrations, helps enhance collaborative work as facilitators.

Be Culturally Sensitive

Try to keep in mind cultural differences in language and slang terms. Some great, commonly used activities have names or use terms that could be offensive or hurtful. The importance of this became clear to me when working in a public school in Wisconsin with a high population of students from a Hmong refugee background. I adapted the name of an activity known as "Mine Field" in many activity books (Rohnke, 1984) to "Cow Pasture" as I knew many of my students from Southeast Asia could find the concept of a minefield very frightening. Also a cow pasture was much more appropriate to the setting of my school in rural Wisconsin!

Allow for Struggle

Sometimes teachers, counselors, or group leaders have a hard time allowing learners to labor through difficult group problems. On the challenge course, I often see adults jump in and try to solve problems for student participants. When this happens, opportunities for students to gain valuable problem-solving skills or take responsibility for the success of the experience are missed.

With that said, there are times when struggling or laboring through the problem becomes too hard, paralyzing the group. John Dewey (1938) referred to this as a "miseducative*" experience. There is a delicate balance between group members' learning from a problem and being paralyzed by frustration. This balance has to be discov-

"The gem cannot be polished without friction, nor man perfected without trials." Confucius

* Miseducative experience: John Dewey(1929) used the terms "miseducative" and "uneducative" to refer to different types of experiences that do not promote education. An experience is miseducative if it interferes or gets in the way of the growth of further experience. For example, if someone finds a challenge course experience too overwhelming or frustrating they might just dismiss it entirely. A miseducative experience is an experience that can limit a person's future growth.

ered and maintained with each group situation as it arises. Effective facilitators are willing to put forward as many questions as answers and allow participants to learn from problems and conflict without jumping too early to help or give answers.

For interesting reading on this subject see Plato's *Theatetus*. In this work, Plato uses the metaphor of the teacher as the "midwife" of ideas. It points out that a midwife acts as a guide and support. She cannot give birth for the mother-to-be; she can only help and encourage. She only intervenes when the situation becomes dangerous or too painful. When learners feel responsible for their learning, they are more empowered to take ownership for future learning, growth, and change.

What Is Success?

The importance of allowing for struggle and helping people learn from challenges needs to be tempered with a realization that "success" looks different for every group. When I provide trainings on challenge course activities and problem-solving games and initiatives, new facilitators often want to know about the level of challenge or "rules" I set with groups. They ask questions like: How strict are you about the parameters of the challenge? Do you make everyone go back on the spider's web if someone touches? What if someone uses their spotter to help; do you make them go back and start over? These are interesting and important questions. I know that my own approach to dealing with these kinds of situations has changed greatly over the years.

When I first entered the challenge course field, it seemed common for facilitators to have very concrete rules for each activity. These rules were not adjusted for specific groups. For example, if a spotter physically helped someone stay on the cable, that person was required to go back and start over. Some groups respond well to this kind of challenge. Other groups might find it extremely frustrating, and it could actually end up in the realm of the "miseducative" experience.

Within a two-week period I facilitated some team building experiences with two different groups of employees from a wholesale grocery distribution company. It was very interesting to see the two groups' perceptions of success on the Spider's Web activity, which involves passing group members through a giant "web" strung between trees without touching the web.

The first group was the warehouse staff. Their jobs in the warehouse required attention to detail and an awareness of safety and exactness. They approached the Spider's Web activity with the kind of precision and care they had to use in their work at the warehouse. They spent over an hour on the initiative. Any time a participant touched the web, the whole group went back and started over. This was the goal they had set with their facilitator. When they finally finished, they were very pleased and able to connect the success back to specific strengths of their team in the workplace.

A week later I worked with the management team from the same company. The warehouse manager who had come with his staff the week before attended this day as a management team member. The small group of management staff was focused on systems, communication, and big-picture ideas for their company. They approached

the Spider's Web differently from the group from the warehouse. When asked to set a goal for completion, they decided to place a stick between a few threads of the web. If anyone touched the web enough to move the stick they would all go back. They were conscious of everyone's safety and practiced excellent communication throughout, carefully planning how they were going to pass each other through the web. There were a few slight touches, but not enough to move the stick, and the group finished in about half an hour.

All the participants were very pleased with their success except the warehouse manager, who felt that they could have raised the bar on perfection. He shared the experience of the warehouse staff and his disappointment that this group's outcome wasn't the same. His peers listened carefully and then asked him to think about the differences between the two groups' job requirements and how that was illustrated in the way each group approached the web. They discussed how the different approaches represented how they should approach their work at the company.

Every group is different, and its needs are different. Letting group members take responsibility for goals and set parameters that are meaningful to them makes the initiative more personal and powerful.

Chapter 5

Facilitation Tricks & Tips

As facilitators gain experience and practice, they develop a repertoire of favorite tricks and tools to enhance their work. These techniques are learned from other facilitators, their group members, workshops, books, and those brilliant accidents inherent to the process of facilitation. The following pages are a collection of some of my favorite simple techniques for adding fun to facilitation, easing transitions from activity to activity, and dealing with challenging group situations.

Dividing Into Teams or Groups

My favorite way to divide participants into groups or teams for an activity is a method that both honors participants' needs for a sense of control and choice over who is going to be their partner, and practices compromise. This method can also help you subtly separate specific participants when needed to mitigate behavior problems and increase diverse interaction. Teachers report that this simple exercise in practicing compromise has helped change their classroom! Adult participants share that they enjoy the sense of connection from sharing and making decisions about these hypothetical scenarios.

- Have everyone grab a partner. Yes, this means they can choose their best buddy. In fact, this can be ideal for this activity. If there is an uneven number in the group, you can step in.

- Have everyone face his or her partner and say hello. Then share an imaginary scenario with the group, such as:

  "Imagine it is summer and the two of you are near a river. You want to play on the river, but the only boats available are a kayak and a one-person canoe. Which one of you will take the kayak and which the canoe?"

  Other scenarios could surround ice cream flavors, roller blades or skateboard, skis or snowshoes, sailboat or speedboat etc.

- The participants have to come to a compromise and decide who will use the kayak and who will use the canoe.

- Then have the "canoes" stand in one spot and the "kayaks" in another, and you have two teams.

- If multiple, smaller groups are needed, repeat the exercise with new partners and different choices until the desired-size groups are reached.

I worked with a 2nd grade teacher on implementing experiential community building into her classroom, spending an hour or so in her classroom leading some cooperative games. Early in the session, I created two groups by having students partner up. I had them imagine that they were at the circus and, after waiting in line for cotton candy, they found only one blue and one pink cotton candy left. The students had to decide who was to get which one. One set of students started arguing about this imaginary decision. I decided to call on another pair who had already decided and asked them how they came to their decision. One student responded, "Well, we both wanted pink, but I am okay with blue, *and* I wanted

 to find out what you were going to have us play, so I let her have the pink one." At that point, I briefly defined compromise to the group. The other pairs decided quickly and quietly at this point, and we moved on to engage in a series of cooperative activities.

"More grows in the garden than the gardener knows he has sown."
Spanish Proverb

Later in the day, the teacher told me that as the students lined up for lunch, a squabble erupted about who was going to lead the line to the cafeteria. Just as she was going to intervene, a little voice from the back of the line said, "You know, this is just like the cotton candy; we all just want to get to lunch." This ended the squabble, and they proceeded to the cafeteria. Sometimes the simple, small things we do as teachers have more of an effect than we realize.

Using Competition

At one point in my career, when I was working with kids in a treatment program, I stopped using competitive games altogether because I was working with kids with many behavior issues who had great difficulty maintaining appropriate behavior during competition. What I realized soon after creating this moratorium on competition was that I was not helping them learn healthy skills. They needed to learn how to compete in a healthy way.

Over the years, I have run into some helpful tricks to keep up the high energy associated with competition but eliminate some of the negative behaviors and model more prosocial interaction. One of those is "Team Switching," a great method that I have used successfully with many groups.

====================================

Break up an activity by having "everyone who has stripes on" or "everyone who has been to Chicago" or "people with summer birthdays" switch teams with someone else. Group participants of all ages seem to enjoy this switching aspect. It adds a little fun and chaos, and pretty soon no one is paying attention to the score—just the game!

Using Group Consensus Activities

consensus: 1. an opinion or position reached by the group as a whole.
2. general agreement or acceptance, approval.

The consensus process not only requires the agreement of most participants, but it also seeks to understand the opinion and viewpoint of dissenters. The aim is to resolve differences through discussion, and come up with the most agreeable decision for the whole group. The value of practicing consensus in the context of developing group processing skills is that consensus is all about quality discussion and embracing and understanding the opinions of those with differing viewpoints. It involves conflict resolution, active listening, and prosocial communication skills. It allows the entire group to take responsibility for the final decision. Polling can be used to test consensus along the way.

Our society is becoming increasingly isolative. Kids aren't out playing pickup games of kickball or kick the can during free time after school or on summer evenings as they once did. Parents are often nervous about letting kids play in their neighborhoods unsupervised by adults. Young people are heavily programmed after school in adult-led activities including sports, clubs, and after-school programs. There is obviously great value in involving kids in these kinds of structured programs. The downfall is that many children are not gaining the skills learned from interaction within peer only groups, such as coming to consensus on the basics of play, deciding who is going to be "it," or whether the ball was in or out of bounds.

I remember as a kid having many opportunities for unstructured play in our neighborhood; pickup games of all kinds filled our summer days and after-school hours. Arguments about who was "it" or who won inevitably arose, but we figured out ways to work it out ourselves rather than interrupt the game to run home and get an adult to intervene.

During playground time at school, today's students go to teachers for help in resolving even the simplest disagreements or conflicts. They even depend on teachers to choose teams and act as referees. It appears that with less participation in peer-only play and more adult-led, structured programs on the agenda, kids are becoming dependent on adults to make decisions for them and are missing out on opportunities to gain conflict resolution, problem-solving, and group-communication skills.

After observing this trend, I intentionally focused on implementing activities that practice the use of decision making by consensus when working with students. I purposefully created situations where participants had to come to agreement on the rules of the game. I use a lot of methods that involve pairs and then groups making simple choices and decisions together and work up to practicing consensus. This is valuable practice for groups of all ages.

Examples of Using Consensus in Group Work

- Divide the group into teams by having participants make choices about hypothetical situations (see pages 91-92).

- Have teams come up with a team name (limit it to a topic like type of car, type of bug, etc.).

- In reflection, use consensus along with props or reflection cards: Have the group decide on one card that best represents what it achieved as a group. The outcomes of using group consensus can be very rich. The process of deciding on just one card involves participants sharing their ideas relating to many different cards and making an argument for their interpretation. The dialogue involved in this process can be quite profound. This method of consensus reflection works surprisingly well even for classroom-size groups. Divide very large groups into sub-groups. Provide each group with a set of cards or objects. Once the sub-groups have made their choices, have them return to the large group and share the object they picked. It can be interesting to compare and contrast the sub-groups' choices.

- Sometimes it is helpful to engage the group in discussion about the differences between consensus and voting, and why and when each process of decision making is used.

I hear people argue the merits of consensus versus voting and whether there is such a thing as "true consensus." My intention here is not to fuel that debate, but to share ideas for increasing involvement in discussions and decision making. I find that with the consensus method of reflection, participants can become so involved in identifying with a card, and making an argument for their card, that they are unaware they are engaging in reflection. When using this method, students who have never shared in a processing discussion speak eloquently about their choice and how it represents the accomplishments and attributes of their group. Try it!

Rock, Paper, Scissors Tag

This game is the macro-version of the common playground activity "Rock, Paper, Scissors" (one of the few child-led decision making activities I still see in schools). I was introduced to this activity first through New Games *put out by the New Games Foundation (Fleugelman, 1976). There are many variations of this game, including one used by environmental education centers that substitutes rock, paper, scissors with salmon, bear, mosquito. Another common version created by Karl Rohnke (1989) uses giants, wizards, elves in the same way.*

Equipment:
Poly spots or other boundary markers

Focus/Content Areas:
Leadership, compromise, consensus, respect, planning, communication, listening, assertiveness, focus, play. I keep coming back to Rock, Paper, Scissors Tag especially when working with kids around practicing interpersonal and leadership skills. This is a method kids use on the playground to practice consensus, so it really seems to hit home when we play it with a purpose! This game can be adapted for small classroom spaces by adding in a rule that players must move in a heel-to-toe walk, which slows everyone down to an appropriate speed for a small space.

Facilitation Suggestions:

- Divide the group into two teams. I use my favorite partner division compromise activity to divide teams (see p. 91-92).

- Using poly spots or other markers, I delineate a middle "face-off" line and two lines on either end of the playing area that represent each team's "safe" area.

- Instruct each team to form a huddle in their safe area and decide as a team whether they are going to be rock, paper, or scissors. Emphasize that they can only be one of these things (i.e., the whole team has to agree on being the same thing). This could be a great lesson on leadership and compromise for your students.

- Also remind players that this is Rock, Paper, Scissors Tag only, and there is no cement, glue, dynamite, or other various alternative (the kids will know what you are talking about).

- Sometimes I have team members come up with an alternate choice in case there is a tie and we want to do a second round.

- After both teams have come to a decision, have them come to the middle face-off area.

- On the count of three, have teams show their signs. The winning team chases the opposing team.

- If a participant is tagged, he is captured and joins the tagging team.

- Groups get caught up in the fun and excitement of this game and will usually eagerly participate in a number of rounds. Sometimes groups will use strategy, luck, or some kind of consensus to end the game. Each group's approach is different and can lead to interesting reflection discussions on decision making, group communication, and consensus.

Outcome/Processing Ideas:
Compromise, decision making, listening, leadership, dealing with frustration, fair play.

One of my most memorable experiences with consensus-focused activities in groups was with a 5th grade group of students in a community building program in their school. I decided to play Rock, Paper, Scissors Tag with this class as a communication builder and a warm-up to another problem-solving activity I had planned. When the students came to the middle to show their signs, one of the teams repeatedly came to middle with all three signs! Clearly they had not agreed at all on a group strategy. I stopped the action and asked the group what was happening. One student spoke up, "I think we need to elect a captain."

Immediately a boy's hand shot up in the air and he exclaimed, "Me, pick me."

The first student knowingly responded, "No, that's not what I meant; I think we should have a captain who will listen to everybody and then make a decision about whether we should be rock, paper, or scissors—not just pick what he wants."

A girl from the other team chimed in saying "NO! No captains!" (It appeared to the teacher and me that she was the self-appointed leader of the other team.)

All of this led to an in-depth discussion by the students around decision making and leadership, and the difference between a democracy and a dictatorship (things they were studying in social studies). They also tied this experience in with a recent school election and how they wanted decisions made in their classroom. As evidenced by the discussion, this activity became much more than just an icebreaker!

The Creative Use of Props

The use of unique props can increase participant interest and engagement. In a team building activity involving throwable objects, the silliness of a rubber chicken, fish, or slug adds a sense of fun, novelty, and interest to the learning situation.

I have a unique old toolbox I found at a flea market a few years ago. This "treasure chest" holds the objects I use for processing with groups. I found that just having the toolbox around without opening it for a while—maybe even a session or two—creates intrigue. Once I open it for a reflection activity, I have the group's full attention.*

---

* This was yet another facilitation trick discovered by accident when I brought the toolbox to a classroom and was not able to use it because plans had changed. When I was finally ready to use it, I had the student's rapt attention and the inspiration to make this trick intentional.

On the challenge course, props can be used to reinforce goal setting. Have the group members choose objects that represent real life personal or group goals. Place the chosen objects at the ending point of a group challenge, and create an opportunity for the group to discuss how the skills used in the activity relate to skills used in real life situations.

It is inspiring for a group to carry an object that represents its success, skills, or goals from activity to activity. These objects act as a reminder of group goals and experience. For example, a group of students I worked with recently on the challenge course chose three body part props (an ear, brain, and hand)* from my treasure chest to represent the three most important skills they used during a difficult activity. The students carried them along to the next challenge. When listening was needed, a student held up the ear, prompting the group to stop talking over each other and listen.

I have also seen groups make use of props in challenging communication situations by spontaneously using the rubber chicken or other object for use as a "talking stick" to help organize communication. Rather than everyone talking at once, the object is passed for individuals to speak in turn.

---

* The body parts processing tool is available from www.Training-Wheels.com, 7095 South Garrison St., Littleton, CO 80128 (888-553-0147).

Props can be creatively used to make activities more inclusive. On the challenge course while facilitating activities that are very physically demanding, I often offer a hoola hoop or rubber poly spot as a "magic spot" that can be used once or twice in a traversing or swinging activity as a stepping stone. This gives group members who might have physical limitations an opportunity to actively participate using an alternative method that allows them to help achieve the group goal. As part of the challenge, I ask the whole group to work together to decide when and how this limited use prop/resource can be used. The decision of where, when, or if the resource gets placed is naturally woven into the challenge and becomes part of the group's strategy, planning, and communication.

I once had an amusing experience when I spontaneously decided to add an assortment of what I thought were silly, unusable props or "red herrings" to the crate of intentional tools I provided for a group to use to solve a problem. The group actually ended up using the red herrings (a roll of toilet paper, a horseshoe, and a dustpan) instead of the carefully measured rope lengths and surgical tubing I had intended them to use. This reinforced for me the joy of acting spontaneously, welcoming the unexpected, and having faith in the creative spirit of groups.

The use of props can spark interest, creativity, and a sense of fun and meaning in facilitation. Keep in mind that any time you add a prop, it is important to consider any safety issues that might arise with the use of that object or tool. For example, if a rope is used as an aid, ensure that knots are tied properly.

Using Blindfolds in Facilitation*

Many facilitators effectively use blindfolds in problem-solving initiatives or group communication activities to add depth and challenge

---

* This section on using blindfolds in facilitation originally appeared in Facilitator's Toolbox in the ACCT newletter, *Parrallel Lines, Summer,* 2001.

to an activity. Blindfolds are used to frame activities around topics such as adaptation, tolerance, individual difference, leadership, trust, and communication. Facilitators often use blindfolds in a challenge course activity such as "the maze" where participants who are blindfolded work together to get through an imaginary maze. A number of engaging activities designed to build communication skills challenge participants to give a blindfolded peer directions to complete a task. Although they can be a useful facilitation tool, blindfolds can be incredibly intimidating to some participants. Along with the emotional safety issue, some youth programs also avoid sharing blindfolds to prevent the spread of lice.

I was faced with this dilemma when I wanted to use blindfolds with a student group. After brainstorming ideas for using and presenting blindfolds in a way that was engaging and positive for participants, I ended up having the students make their own.

The students were assigned to create and construct a blindfold using materials from home. They received prizes for categories such as most creative, most reliable, most colorful, etc. (with everyone receiving a prize of some kind). The blindfold creations ranged from "shades" made solely from duct tape, to swim goggles painted in gold, to a football helmet colorfully decorated along the lines of a space creature. The students not only ended up with their own blindfold for the semester, but had fun using their creativity. It was a great way for them to expressive themselves in the group,

Other colorful options for blindfolds are Mardi Gras style masks and painted sunglasses. I have noticed participants are more comfortable with colorful blindfolds than dark strips. Some programs just have participants close their eyes.

and they had a lasting memento of their course to take home. Although this may not be realistic for one-day programs, it could work for camps, treatment, and other multiple-day programs.

Another suggestion given to me by a participant in a workshop a few years ago was the idea of giving participants in long-term programs a bandana of their own at the start of the program, with the intention that they keep the bandana and use it throughout the program.

This bandana idea could be combined with an interesting processing/introduction activity I learned during my time at the University of New Hampshire. Have participants choose a bandana that best represents their personality from an assortment of different styles, designs, and colors. The bandana then becomes a tool for them to use for the program and a memento of their experience. This activity can also be used to close a group. Group members choose and present bandanas to each individual at the end of the program based on what the group feels best represents that peer's strengths, achievements, and positive qualities.[*]

The way we as facilitators frame the use of blindfolds plays an important role in our participants' reactions. I usually tell participants that blindfolds are just a reminder to keep their eyes closed. Regardless of the kind of blindfolds your program uses, remember the importance of giving participants a choice over what they participate in. USING A BLINDFOLD SHOULD ALWAYS BE A CHOICE. Never

---

[*] To read more about the bandana processing activity, see *Reflective Learning, Theory and Practice* by Sugarman, Doherty, Garvey, & Gass.

tie the blindfold on a participant unless they ask for help. The goal is to make the experience emotionally safe and empowering.

Many facilitators choose not to use blindfolds at all and just trust participants to close their eyes for the activity. I find I am doing this more, as it gives group members a choice to participate at the level they are ready for. Participants who peek probably would have with blindfolds too.

Using Popular Culture

People of all ages find humor, relevance, and metaphors for learning in popular culture. I have found great success and fun using popular culture in the facilitation of problem-solving initiatives and other activities with groups. Participants appreciate the effort made to connect to their "real world." When using ideas from popular culture with student groups, I have even had youth express appreciation for meeting them where they are, and entering their world for a change.

Creatively weaving references to popular culture into group activities can expand the use of metaphor and transference of learning. It helps increase the connection from the learning activity to outside experiences. It can liven up your work as a facilitator, and most importantly, it is fun. Including popular references is a way of celebrating the humor and creativity that exists in our culture.

An opportunity to integrate pop culture into an activity arose when I was presenting a commonly known problem-solving challenge called "Toxic Waste" or "Nuclear Reactor" to high school students. In this activity, the group is given the hypothetical task of shutting down a nuclear reactor core (actually a bucket of ping-pong balls

---

* For those who aren't familiar, the fictional locale of the Simpson family is the town of Springfield, home of a nuclear power plant that is often involved in a storyline of eminent peril and positive resolution.

and marbles in the center of a circle). I decided to call the activity "Saving Springfield" in reference to the popular TV show *The Simpsons*.* The students immediately engaged in the fun theme.

The recent popularity of TV reality shows has brought an increased interest in group challenge activities. A number of years ago when the TV show *Survivor* first appeared, I engaged a group of high school students who were part of a semester-long challenge course class in an activity that involved a variety of problem-solving elements and physical challenges. The students started creatively imbedding references to the *Survivor* show into the activity, which added intrigue, enjoyment, and increased buy-in from more reluctant group members. One student wrote the following in his journal:

> *"Every time I go to class now, I think of our group more like one of those Survivor groups. As the days go by, we learn a little more about each other, leaders step up, and we develop a way to solve all of these corny little problems. It's kind of fun and not like other classes.*

> *"I've noticed lately that I've gotten a lot more talkative. I don't know if that has anything to do with this class, but the effects are definitely showing. I'm more social, and therefore happier and more successful at getting my ideas across. I'm not really a leader in the group, but I'm definitely playing a key role. I am confident I won't be voted off the 'island' any time soon."*

Have fun as you facilitate and key into the popular culture references you hear from participants, using them when the appropriate opportunities arise. People will appreciate the humor and relevancy of the lessons. These efforts can help learners engage more readily in activities and may synthesize lessons in a way that is meaningful to them.

Chapter 6

Creating Meaning:
Reflection & Metaphor

The essential element of experiential education is to help participants grow and change and create meaningful and lasting lessons
from their group experiences. Facilitators can create opportunities for learners to make connections from the skills they use in a
"contrived environment" (such as a classroom, challenge course,
corporate training, or therapeutic group session) to real life issues
such as resolving conflicts with peers, dealing with frustration,
expressing their opinions, or setting goals and priorities.

Traditionally facilitators have used verbal methods to review and
reflect on experiences, reinforce lessons, and/or help the group define meaning in an experience. This often involved a facilitator-led
question-and-answer session following the experience. Although
there is value in group discussion and insight from the facilitator,
this approach has its limitations. Many participants and facilitators are intimidated by this kind of verbal discussion, especially at
first. There are many innovative ways to engage a group in dialogue and reflection kinesthetically, emotionally, and socially that
aren't dependent on the facilitator's leading a didactic question-
and-answer session.

There is no set way to facilitate reflection or a perfect time during
group development to process experience. Facilitators can weave
in the opportunities for creating meaning and connection as part
of the activity or initiative itself. Good facilitators learn to read
their group, use a variety of techniques, and look for opportunities

to reinforce key learnings as they are happening. The most engaging and effective way of reflecting is to use activities that give learners the power to take the lead in reflection.

Helping facilitators develop tools and methods for facilitating processing has become a passion and focus of my work over the past 10 years. In the process of sharing ideas with other facilitators at conferences, I connected with two talented practitioners, Steven Simpson of the University of Wisconsin–LaCrosse and Michelle Cummings of Training Wheels Inc. They have helped me view processing in a whole new way and develop a repertoire of activities that reach learners in meaningful and in-depth ways. These facilitators share my passion for facilitating reflective practice with groups, and they have created a number of interesting tools and techniques for reflection and using metaphor to enhance learning.

My view on processing changed dramatically in 1997 when I was first introduced to the idea of participant-directed processing through the work of Steven Simpson, Buzz Bocher, and Dan Miller. They put forward the idea of using reflective tools (like Chiji Cards, Chiji Dice, and Chiji Pocket Processor) that aim to move more of the responsibility for reflection from the facilitator into the hands of the participants.

"There are two great regions in which the life of every person resides. They are the region of action and the region of thought. It is impossible to separate these two regions from one another and to bid one man live in them alone and the other man live only in the other of them."
Phillips Brooks

I started experimenting with methods that give more freedom and control over learning to participants, such as integrating activity and discussion and using symbolic methods. I then met Michelle Cummings and we connected through our shared enthusiasm for participant-centered processing methods. Over the past decade, she and I have shared a variety of processing tools with facilitators, hoping to inspire them with this new perspective on reflection. The methods we have found useful range from metaphorical symbols and props to kinesthetic movement during discussion to journaling and artwork. This collaboration culminated in a book project with Jim Cain, a creative facilitator and founder of Teamwork Teamplay entitled *A Teachable Moment: A Facilitator's Guide to Activities for Processing, Debriefing, Reviewing and Reflection*. This book is based on the idea that facilitators will engage groups more readily when they mix up their methods. Participant-centered techniques are presented to involve people in a variety of ways to meet varying learning styles and build comfort with reflective practice. The activities mentioned in the following pages are some of my personal favorites. Many can be found in a more detailed version in *A Teachable Moment*.

Remember processing doesn't always have to take place after an activity is over. Some of the best reflection can happen DURING the activity. Use a "stop action" to pause the group mid-activity and take a look around to see what is happening. This is an effective tool to use when conflict or frustration levels are high, but remember to use it when the group is working well together. Celebrate successes!

As you explore these activities, keep in mind your own attitudes about reflection and how you approach this aspect of group facilitation. Participants really respond to your cues—if you approach reflection as an exciting and enjoyable activity rather than that "tedious thing you have to do" at the end of an activity, participants will be likely to perceive it positively too.

It is important to carefully sequence reflective activities to achieve optimal outcomes. Often facilitators get caught in the trap of asking in-depth questions about participants' feelings and reactions before the group has learned to be comfortable sharing and reflecting together. Be creative in implementing reflective activities. Processing doesn't have to happen at the end of an activity. In a conversation at a conference, a facilitator from Belgium once told me that in his program they rarely reflect at the end of an activity. Instead he involves participants in reflecting during the activity, in the midst of the action, where he believes reflection is most meaningful. I have tried this strategy and found it effective.

As you facilitate reflection, be open to experimentation, and learn from your participants. Participant-centered methods can add a sense of fun and interest to reflection and great value and meaning to group experiences.

The Art of Reflective Conversation

These tips will help you create an environment that encourages involvement in meaningful reflection and discussion.

- Create a circular space to best position the group for sharing.

- Remember the importance of the physical environment and be cognizant of possible distractions: temperature, time of day, seating, etc.

- Reinforce the importance of "active listening" or being "fully present."

- Allow group members to pass during discussions. This empowers them to have control over their learning and practice sharing at their own pace. When participants are given the power to pass, they learn to trust the facilitator and group and often end up offering a great deal to the group at their own pace.

- Allow for some superficial answers or comments in group discussions, especially in the beginning stages of group development. Remember that reflective discussions take practice.

- Silences are okay. They are even necessary. Allow group members to think and formulate their ideas before rushing on to the next topic. Participants can be experiencing valuable reflection even if they don't share it with the group.

- Be prepared for group members to take discussions somewhere different than you had in mind. You might learn something new! **Be prepared to artfully help individuals navigate back to the present moment in order to meet the needs of the group.**

- Mix up your methods. Variety is not only the spice of life but, according to new scientific brain research, novelty (and the use of different learning tools and methods) facilitates learning.

- Practice reflection. Reflecting on our own practice as facilitators enhances our learning, i.e., what works and what doesn't, and helps us see the benefit of our programs.

- Give control to participants; do not force your agenda on them. Be flexible. Let them take responsibility for their learning and their interpretation of an experience during group discussion.

- The facilitator doesn't have to hear everything said in group for it to be effective. Try activities that do not involve the facilitator by dividing the group into smaller reflection groups.

- Use open-ended questions. Summarize or restate what was said, or, even better, have a group member restate the discussion.

- Closure is important. Be thoughtful about how you end a program or day's experience. Think about what you want the group to leave with. Carefully design a closing activity that helps group members tie their learning together and encourages future learning.

- Never forget the importance of humor, but remember the difference between humor and sarcasm.

- Be attentive to when it is time to move on, even if you have to let go of some of your facilitation goals for the discussion.

- When questions come to you as the facilitator, try to direct them back to the group, letting group members help each other.

Twists on the Traditional Sharing Circle

The following are some ways to ease a group into conversation and help participants increase their comfort level and reflective skills in a sequential fashion. These techniques introduce group members to the idea of combining action and reflection and help them get comfortable sharing in simple, concrete ways. Starting the reflective process in this way increases a group's comfort level with processing and leads to more in-depth reflection and discussions as the group members progress in their development together. When you facilitate group discussions formally, allow group members to pass, especially at first. This helps participants feel empowered to share when they are ready, rather than to please others. Some participants reflect quietly, while others are more comfortable verbalizing their feelings during discussion. Remember, reflection is a skill that is developed with practice; people get more comfortable if processing activities are thoughtfully sequenced and they feel empowered by having choice and control over when they share.

One-Word Reaction

This is a simple way to get group members comfortable with group processing.

Facilitation Suggestions:

- After an activity (even an introductory icebreaker), ask group members to go around the circle and share a one-word reaction to the activity. Ask them not to think about it too much, just to share their first, one-word thought.

- Give participants an opportunity to pass. This is imperative to building comfort and trust in a group that is developing its reflective and conversational skills.

- In this activity, it doesn't matter if the word is the same as someone else's or seems superficial. The purpose is to practice sharing and build comfort and trust at this point.

Top Three Skills

This is a simple task that just takes a few moments and starts the reflective and sharing process.

- Following an activity, have the group name three things it did well as a group during the activity.

Skills Lists

When I work with a group of students who are intimidated by processing, I find that simply asking them to brainstorm a list of the skills they used in an activity can be a helpful way to engage them in a non-threatening way. This may be the first time that they have been formally asked to recognize the strengths and skills they bring to the group. This method is also helpful for visual learners.

Facilitation Suggestions:

- Provide group members with a flip chart or other large writing surface and markers and ask them to create a list of the skills they used during the activity.

- Use this skill's list to help frame future activities in the program.

- The skill's list can be combined with other reflection activities to help participants connect the skills used in a group game or initiative to real life situations.

Stop Action

Some facilitators believe the best reflection is actually done DURING an activity while emotions are high and there is maximum focus. Processing or reviewing done later might miss some teachable moments. Sometimes a group will experience a pivotal teachable moment in the middle of a problem-solving initiative. Brain-based research has shown that immediate feedback and reflection can be valuable (Jensen, 2004).

- In the midst of an activity, "freeze" the group. Ask if anyone can share what is happening with the group at that moment.

- When you get one or two answers continue with the activity.

- Remember to stop action to celebrate positive as well as difficult moments.

Simple Evaluation

- Have the group name one thing it did very well and one thing it might do differently next time.

Partner Sharing

A number of popular introductory activities can also be used for reflection. Try using your favorite icebreaker or warm-up activities. Earlier in this book, I presented a few partner introduction activities such as "Handshake Mingle" and "Concentric Circles" that could be used for reflecting as well as introductions. The value of reflecting with partners or in small groups is that par-

ticipants are often more open if they aren't speaking to the facilitator or the group as a whole. These kinesthetic partner activities used as processing can be less threatening for participants than a traditional sharing circle, and they are interactive and fun. Remember good processing can happen even if the facilitator is not present to hear it.

Facilitation Suggestions:

- As with the introduction activity outlined earlier, divide the group in half and form two circles with the participants in an inner circle and an outer circle, facing each other.

- Have participants greet each other, do an activity together, and answer a question asked by the facilitator about the activity or experience the group is processing.

- Switch partners by having the inner group move to the left three spaces.

- Have participants greet their new partner, do an activity, share their answers to the facilitator's question, and switch partners again. And so on.

Questions with the Roll of a Dice

I have found some engaging reflective activities that use dice as question prompts for groups. These are very effective in getting groups to talk about their experiences. The randomness of the roll of the dice adds a sense of fun that increases participation from even the most reluctant members of a group. (Dice can also be used to pick questions for journaling or sharing in pairs.)

Michelle Cummings of Training Wheels Inc. created the "processing cube," a large, colorful cube

with pockets. Laminated
question cards can be slid
into the pockets, allowing
many opportunities for variations (see resource list).

Steven Simpson, Dan Miller,
and Buzz Bocher of the
Institute for Experiential
Education created the Chiji
Processing Dice, which in-
cludes four dice. One is marked with arrows and other directions
for WHO will answer the question. The other three have questions
about what happened during the activity, how participants reacted,
and how it all relates to real life.

I have great results using this method with middle and high school
students. Each of the students wants a turn rolling the dice—
which actually means more questions on which to reflect. They
don't seem to mind this at all. Groups perceive this as a fun and
engaging activity rather than "work" done after the activity.

Creating Meaning With Metaphor

Since the beginning of civilization humans have expressed themselves through symbols. Often people can more easily express
themselves through a symbol or picture than through verbal
means. Symbols spark feelings (Takahashi, 1995) and work to
make feelings outwardly discussable and objectively real (Sandelands, 1998). Symbols help people communicate and share their
frames of thought. They can help people understand abstract
concepts that cannot always be translated into words.

Image cards, pictures, artwork, and tangible objects can be used
as meaningful and engaging tools for facilitating reflection, goal
setting, creating group norms, resolving conflict, and celebrat-

ing individual and group strengths and positive attributes. Brain research suggests that using metaphors and symbols helps cement lessons and transfer learning to everyday life (Sousa, 2006; Jensen, 2004).

My collection of postcards, image cards, and interesting objects is invaluable for prompting group discussion and reflection. As mentioned throughout this book, I use these tools in a variety of ways—for introducing groups and goal setting at the start of a program, helping to establish group norms and identifying the qualities of a positive group environment, and resolving difficult group situations. All of these tools are especially useful in reflection or processing with a group.

These methods are effective because participants can attach their thoughts to an object that can be touched and shown to a group. Because the participants can talk about the object or image rather than about themselves directly, they sometimes express thoughts that would otherwise be left unsaid. When groups use pictures and objects in group discussions, the thoughts, ideas, and connections seem broader and deeper than when using dialogue alone.

Participants who are normally reticent about sharing seem more comfortable when they can attach their thoughts to an object.

"Metaphor thus has the intriguing attribute of having two central but opposing roles. On the one hand, it promotes greater clarity in what is said, while, on the other, it serves as a shielded form of discourse."
Graham Low

These methods are not only engaging and non-threatening; they allow abundant opportunities for creative, spontaneous, and meaningful interpretation of an experience. A visual representation of an experience can be effective long after the experience is over, reminding a group or participant of the key lessons learned.

When groups agree on an object or symbol that represents their collective experience, this symbol can end up carrying a great deal of power for a group (Cain, Cummings, & Stanchfield, 2005, p. 42). Remember the example of "the turtles" in chapter two of this book. A drawing or collaboratively created symbol can become a kind of mascot representing the group's strengths and achievements, or represent a goal to be reached. Younger participants also can benefit from the use of symbols in facilitation; I find that children naturally think in metaphors because they are accustomed to storytelling and using their imaginations in this way.

These object or picture card methods are useful as introductory activities, for processing reactions to a specific experience, for closure, or even as tools to help participants resolve conflict. Although both the image and object activities are similar approaches, I find that groups respond differently to using cards or pictures than they do objects. You can present both object and picture activities in a program and they won't be perceived as a repeated activity; they actually will reach people in different ways.

Using Pictures and/or Objects in Reflection

- Ask the group to come to consensus on one card/object that best represents their experience as a group, the strengths of the group, or something they have achieved.

- Have the group pick three objects or images that represent three important skills they used in the activity that they think will be useful in upcoming activities. Have them carry these objects with them to the next activity, and find a way to integrate them into the next activity or refer back to them to illustrate transfer of skills/learning to future situations.

- Group members can use cards/objects to relate the "story" of their experience by lining up four or five cards/objects that demonstrate how they progressed through the activity, the day, or the course as a whole.

- Participants can each pick their own card/object and then draw or write about it in their journals.

- Groups respond differently to using cards or pictures than they do to using objects, even though they are similar approaches. When facilitators mix up their methods, they reach different learning styles.

- In some situations, it could be appropriate for group members to choose a symbol/object for another person in the group as a memento or gift representing the strengths or contributions that person lent to the experience.

- Consider allowing participants to keep the charm that represents their strength or achievement as a memento/reminder.

- Use your creativity; the possibilities for this type of activity are endless.

Miniature Metaphors

This has become a favorite metaphoric processing tool. Like other object and image activities, I use it for introductions, reflection, and for group closure. The small charms and objects become tangible symbols and metaphors for experience. For years Michelle and I shared our treasure chests (Cain et al., 2005) at workshops and conferences. My original "treasure chest" is a large, old toolbox. Often outdoor educators would ask us, "Do you have smaller processing tools that I could take into the field with me?" Inspired by this question, I found small charms at a local bead store, placed them in a tin, and started using Miniature Metaphor activities.*

Memento of Experience

When people leave a group program with an object representing their experience, they physically carry away a piece of the lesson learned. Every time they see this memento it is a tangible reminder of the knowledge gained from the experience. With this in mind, you may want to give participants an opportunity to make or choose a "take-away" or "gift" that represents their experience together as a group or as an individual symbol of success. This is a great way to infuse learning experiences into day-to-day life.

In the past, I rarely thought ahead of time to formally offer mementos to group members. However, unplanned opportunities to spontaneously offer a memento of experience have had profound results. These positive results made it seem worth preplanning take-aways in future group experiences.

For example, I recently worked with a group in a three-day challenge course skills training. I decided in advance that as a closing

"A mind that is stretched by a new experience can never go back to its old dimensions."
Oliver Wendall Holmes

---

* Miniature Metaphors processing kits are available through Jen Stanchfield. Visit her website: www.experientialtools.com or call: 802-348-6390.

activity, I would have group members choose a charm (a small metaphoric object) from my Miniature Metaphors tin (processing kit) to represent their experience. Unfortunately, three of the group members had to leave before we participated in our closing activity.

As part of the activity, I asked participants to share with the group why they chose their particular charm. Then, on a whim, I told the group members that I wanted them to keep their charms as a memento of their experience. I asked them, as a group, to choose charms to present to each of their missing colleagues, based on their strengths and contributions to the group. It was quite moving to hear the things group members shared about the charms they chose for their peers. They were very excited about the idea of presenting these gifts to their colleagues. It felt like these participants who had to leave were able, in some fashion, to take part in the closing activity.

Another experience with mementos happened with a group that came to an adventure facilitation workshop. It was a small group that readily bonded and had a very positive and intense experience together. As a closing activity, I had them choose a pewter stone from my processing tool kit. These stones had words engraved on them such as "creativity," "strength," and "empower." Again on a whim, I told the participants to keep their stones as a memento of their experience. They were very pleased with this idea.

A week later, I was at an Association for Experiential Education (AEE) conference in Minneapolis/St. Paul, and during a work-

shop where I was presenting on processing tools, I mentioned using the stones. Aimee Desrosier Cochran, a participant who had attended a previous workshop of mine, was also attending the AEE workshop. She spoke up and shared that she had made a necklace from the stone she had taken as a memento of her experience. She explained that she had stopped at a bead store on her way home from the workshop just to get the tools to make her necklace. This experience reinforced for me how powerful a simple reminder can be.

Three years later, I asked Aimee if she remembered why she picked that stone. She said, "Of course I remember! Why else would I wear it? It helps remind me that I have found what I want to do." She continued to tell me that when she came to that workshop, she had just changed to the outdoor recreation major at Springfield College. She had been facilitating at their challenge course, so the course manager sent her to the workshop. She chose the stone that had "dream" engraved on it as her memento. She shared, "I didn't know what I wanted to do in life, and the group experience during the adventure facilitation workshop helped me know this was my path."

Found Objects

Another variation of the last two reflection methods uses found objects from the natural or classroom environment—eliminating the need for the facilitator to bring props. Have participants select an object from the local environment that represents their role, experience, or successes. You might have to remind them to choose objects that won't harm the natural environment or affect the group members' safety.

Artwork in Reflection

Artistic Expression as Reflective Practice

There is great power in the creation of symbols to represent feelings and experiences. Humans have been creating symbols for experience since the beginning of time. Involvement in individual/group art activities can be a rich, reflective process for participants. The learners end up with a tangible reminder of the learning.

Creating one's own symbol of experience and/or collaborating on the creation of a group symbol has the potential of adding depth and breadth to the initial experience as well as providing a powerful reminder. As mentioned in chapter three, when a symbol is used or created for reflection it leaves the opportunities for meaningful interpretation of an experience wide open. It is a great example of a participant-directed processing activity.

Artistic reflection activities can involve a range of mediums and methods. One activity might involve a drawing that represents a personal or group experience done individually or in collaboration with others. Others could involve sculpture, performance art, photography, music, or documentary—the possibilities are endless. As long as the emphasis is taken off artistic skill, most people will readily engage in this kind of creative activity regardless of their perceptions about their artistic ability. Enhance the process by providing accessible tools and a variety of fun materials and giving short periods of time in a casual atmosphere.

Ideas for Using Art in Reflection

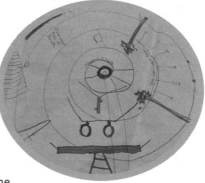

- Involve participants in **creating a picture of their experiences**. This could be part of a formal journaling assignment or a playful group activity. Have participants use any or all of a variety of mediums (paint, crayon, markers, chalk, etc.) and present their art as a story board, cartoon, map, etc. depicting the events of the program. My favorite version of this is to have the group (or small teams within a larger group) create the picture together.

- Ask the group to **create a symbol** that represents its experience and achievements. Again, you could supply a variety of materials (or let them come up with their own) for this project.

- In schools and other longer-term programs, groups can create a **collage or mural** of experience, using a combination of quotes and photographs from the experience (pictures and quotes cut from magazines, etc. could be an option).

- The **community puzzle pieces** mentioned previously can be decorated with representations of each person's strengths and fit together to create a quilt-like mural representing the group's strengths and diversity.

- **Scrapbooking** can incorporate a variety of artistic methods. A student in one of my semester-long challenge course programs created a beautiful scrapbook depicting the group's experience and growth. She used a combination of quotes from fellow students, photographs of their experience, drawings from group members, and found objects.

- There are numerous ways to involve students in **creative writing**. Groups can create a poem or song about their experience. This happened spontaneously a few years ago when a group of students came to a two-day challenge course program. On day two they asked to show me and the other facilitator something. They went right into a rap performance they had created about their experiences on the challenge course the previous day and their requests and expectations for the rest of the program!

"The activity was symbolic, a metaphor for life. It was a right-brain experience that would stick in the unconscious and conscious mind forever." Unknown

Participants can journal about their experience (see upcoming section) or create a story. They could be asked to act as reporters for a newspaper and interview fellow participants.

- **Audio or video documentary** is another challenging art medium. As a graduate student, I worked with students to create an audio recording of a semester-long challenge course class. The compilation CD included snippets of the group's dialogue while involved in an intense problem-solving situation and the laughter and celebration as a peer pushed her comfort zone to jump for a trapeze on the challenge course. Another student created a video documenting the group's progress. The process of editing down and choosing the footage to include was a masterpiece of reflection practice.

- Experiment with the possibilities of using **performance art** as reflection, and your group may go places you never expected. I've seen some interesting group closing activities involving short skits, living sculptures, and even modern dance presentation.

  Michelle Cummings of Training Wheels Inc. often closes a group with an activity she calls "virtual slide show." With each press of a clicker, a different group member volunteers to describe a "picture" of an important moment from their experience. A variation involves group members' creating a short skit/acting out an "instant replay" of an important moment from the day.

Journaling

Time spent reflecting alone, away from the group, balances and supports the group process. It gives learners opportunity to reflect on issues that might not have come up during a group discussion or that they might not feel comfortable verbally expressing in a group setting. Opportunities for individual reflection activities away from group time ensure that reflection is happening regardless of what happens during program time. Journaling and other self-reflective methods can become lifelong skills that help develop insight, one of the hardest skills to learn, but one of the most valuable skills in life.

Journaling is an effective reflection activity that can be used with almost every kind of program in some way. Whether participants are elementary school students or adults, involved in multi-day programs or one-day experiences, journaling can be an incredibly valuable, reflective tool. It can involve a variety of mediums including writing, worksheets, drawings, scrapbooking, photography, and audio or video documentary. Journaling gives learners a tangible memoir of their experience and growth.

Journaling can provide time for reflection that might not be available during the actual program time. Facilitators of school-based and therapeutic programs may have difficulty trying to fit experiential problem-solving activities into a traditional class or group time period. Processing is often sacrificed because of this time crunch. Journaling time or assignments provide opportunities for participants to reflect.

Facilitators who use journaling as a part of long-term programming report that participants demonstrate increased insightful thinking and improved writing skills from their practice of journaling. When journals are shared, they can give participants and facilitators an understanding of group development, the benefits of activities, and feedback about the progression of the group and program.

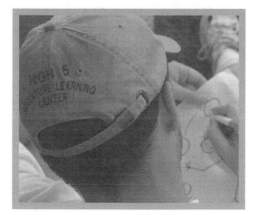

"Rest is much more than bodily relaxation. Like a pause in the music, it affords the opportunity for one to catch up with what is going on."
Unknown

An interesting and easy style of journaling that works well for day programs involves using a sheet of prepared questions with fun spaces provided for the participant to write/draw their answers. This is far less intimidating than a blank page. I found a great example for this type of journaling in *The Me I See* (see resources).

Some Creative Ways to Implement Journaling:

- Create opportunities for participants to make their own journals.

- Include artwork as a part of journaling. Some are more comfortable using artistic representations of their experience.

- Give beginners specific questions to answer to aid the process.

- Have learners create scrapbooks.

- Coordinate with the art department of your school or program to collaborate on projects using alternative forms of media for journaling—such as photography and video and audio documentation.

One of the highlights of my career involved using journaling as part of the facilitation of a semester-long, high school challenge course class. The students' journals shared so much about the value of experiential education—which I intuitively had always known, but was reinforced through their testimonials. It was an inspiring practice for the students, my coteacher Donna Richter, and me. There is more about how we used the journaling information as an evaluative tool in the following chapter.

Sample Journaling Assignment

The following is an example of the journaling that Donna Richter and I assigned to the physical education students who were involved in our semester-long challenge course class.

Example of facilitator's explanation/instructions to the students:

"One of the principles of experiential and adventure education is that of action and reflection. It is an idea presented by the educational philosopher John Dewey. He believed that humans don't truly learn from an experience until they spend some time reflecting and analyzing how the experience is meaningful and relevant to their life. We hope this course will be interesting and fun, and that the skills taught here will be relevant to your life both inside and outside of school.

"The journaling process can help make this class something that will be meaningful and relevant now and in the future. It will give you a record of the work you put into this course, the skills you have learned, and the changes you have made. It is a way for you to take control of your learning and the nature of this course.

"Your writing should reflect your reactions to activities and their relevance to other aspects in life. We want to see more than just a description of what happened in class. We want you to focus on the 'So what?' and 'Now what?' We will give you specific questions and assignments to help guide the process. There are no right or wrong answers in journaling—your grade will be based on participation and effort, so give honest reactions and opinions about your experiences.

"The journal assignment fills the writing requirement for physical education. It amounts to 20% of your grade. Journals will be graded on a five-point scale. You receive one point for handing your journal assignments in and on time. You will receive a point for presentation and effort, for example, having a neat presentation and/or using a notebook or binder. The other three points will be based on the content of your journals, including your answering of questions and writing about your reactions.

"You will receive questions and more specific assignments to help you with your journaling as the semester progresses."

The following general questions are examples of what participants could address in their journal assignments:

- What were your feelings during the activity?

- What did you like and dislike about the activity?

- What were some of the statements you were telling yourself during the activity?

- Were you uncomfortable doing anything? If so, what?

- Were any of your reactions typical of you?

- How do experiences in class relate to other aspects of your life?

Some questions students were given throughout the semester:

Reactions to Spotting Skills Development
- What is healthy trust?

- Is your group trustworthy? How do they show it?

- Was it easy for you to trust the group?

Specific Challenge Course Activities
- What was the experience like?

- What is familiar/different?

- How did your body feel?

- Do you have any goals you plan to set regarding the traverse? Do you feel successful?

- What was most challenging about the activity?

Problem-Solving Activities
- What worked well? What could your group have done differently?

- Did anyone emerge as a leader in your group?

- What role did you play in the group?

- How was your frustration level?

- How were decisions made in this activity?

- What did you like about how the group made decisions? Explain.

- Did you see any positive changes in the group or anybody do something that stands out in your mind?

- Did you learn anything new about yourself or someone else?

- Did you try something you never thought you would?

- Is it easy for you to work with others?

- Do you see any connection between what happened today and home, work, or other school classes?

- What have you learned that may help you in the future?

- What was a highlight for you?

- Did this activity remind you of anything?

As we went into our second and third quarter together, Donna and I expanded this journaling project to involve other media. We teamed up with the computer technology and art teachers to give students other opportunities to record their experience besides writing. One student created a video documentary of our class's experiences. (Each student that quarter received a CD of the class.) Other students created scrapbooks and photo journals. We observed that the students actually ended up putting far more time and energy into processing, reviewing, and reflecting on the class experiences through the video and photo editing process than we could have imagined.

During the second quarter, based on feedback from some of our students who had shared that they struggled with "knowing what to write," we decided to structure the journal assignment differently, giving students specific questions to help them direct their comments. By the end of the second quarter, we observed that the loose structure of the first quarter assignment—when we asked only that participants cover what happened, their reactions to it, and how it might relate to real life—was more productive. Although students struggled at times, they were much more expansive and insightful in their journals than the second quarter class. The second quarter students' writing seemed more superficial and was limited by answering only the questions we gave them. As a result of this observation, Donna adjusted the assignment again for the third quarter class, offering ideas for students, but allowing for creativity in writing. Excerpts from this assignment are on the following page.

Many teachers I have worked with since that first experiment have found great success using journaling with their students. Kim Bohannon of Bridgeport Public Schools in Bridgeport Connecticut shared, "It is a class of only 12 students, and they have done some truly amazing things together. The thoughts they are sharing in their journals are very powerful. This is the class with the student I have been mentioning to you that I have been concerned about (overweight, very low motor skills, disengaged, no friends). What she has accomplished with the help of her peers has been nothing short of magical and miraculous. Her journal entries almost bring me to tears (she has even named her journal!)"

Student Journal Excerpts

Here are a few of the many journal entries students have shared that demonstrate the power of experiential learning.

"I am starting to see why we are doing all of the icebreakers. Over the past week they have helped me get to know my classmates. In the drawing activity, my partner and I found our new language, and communication is very important for the success of our class."

"I feel that I am already starting to know people in the class who I had not talked to in the past, which gives me more confidence to be able to express myself and the ideas and opinions I have."

"The planets game was very cool. At first we were not getting the 'only rule is to have your feet in.' I think we have a tendency to make up a lot of rules. We get trapped into ideas that we make up, just like in real life. We do this in our everyday life by making up societal rules that don't exist."

"The good thing about the holding hand games with the rubber chicken was that it broke the touching borders. We are going to have to get past the awkwardness of touching each other. There are going to be situations where we have to touch someone in order to help them on the ropes course, and I know that some people are more sensitive to touching than others, so they are going to have to get over their fear."

Facilitator Journals

Journaling is of great value for facilitators as well as participants. A logbook of activity agendas and outcomes, including your thoughts and reactions, can be an important resource for evaluating your program's effectiveness, planning future groups, and developing curriculum and action research.

Routinely reflecting and recording group work helps the facilitator gain meaningful insights into developing style, skills, and new activities and approaches. It is good for us sometimes to participate in what we ask our group members to do!

Hopefully some of the activities I have shared will inspire perspectives on the art of facilitation and some new ways of approaching reflection with your groups. Ideally they will help participants become more comfortable with processing and reflection, giving them important practice with creating meaning from experience and developing insight skills that will help them in all aspects of life. As you try them, have fun, and be creative and open to the places a participant-centered approach will take your groups.

The Icing on the Cake

Just as important as starting a program off on the right foot is taking the time to plan and implement reflective and celebratory activities to close the program in a meaningful way. A quality closing activity creates the opportunity to celebrate the group's experience together and recognize individual and group accomplishments. It helps imprint the memory of what the group learned together so participants can carry the learning forward to future experiences and other life situations. It can also be an opportunity for learners to identify the next steps in their learning and any commitments they are making to the group to move forward group or individual goals. I have some favorite tried and true activities I regularly use to bring the group together at the end of a program. Many of these activities are the same ones I used earlier in the program with a different twist.

For large groups, active groups, and when there is little time for a closing, I often use one of the kinesthetic introductory activities such as Concentric Circles or Handshake Mingle that the group experienced earlier as an icebreaker. In the reflective version, I have the original partners from the start of the program revisit each other with a goodbye wish and/or to respond to closing questions. They can combine the fun greetings or handshakes with questions that reflect on the group or individual experiences: "What was a

moment that stood out for you?" "Was there a point when you were frustrated?" "Can you think of a time when you smiled today?" "What is something you will take away from this experience?"

Other active ice breaking activities such as Have You Ever can be used as a closing by changing the question from "Have you ever?" to "Did you experience?" or "Anyone who?" For example, the middle person would ask: "Anyone who tried something new today?" or "Anyone who helped someone today?" Some fun examples of this kind of closing are the Celebrations and Shuffle/Stop/Share/Go activities.

Celebrations

This interactive and fun activity is often used as an icebreaker to discover and celebrate commonalities between participants. In this group closing version we celebrate achievements, highlights, successes, teachable moments, and "take-aways" from the program.

Facilitation Suggestions:

- Have the group stand in a circle.

- Teach the group a short cheer: two leg slaps, two claps, two snaps, and a yeah (with pointer fingers drawn).

- Once participants have mastered the cheer, tell the group that when you call out a thought or experience from the group's time together, anyone who shares this thought or experience should come to the middle to participate in the cheer. Example experiences: "Anyone who helped someone else today." "Anyone who tried something new." "Anyone who was challenged."

- Ask group members to call out their own thoughts and moments from the day.

- End on a positive note, bringing everyone into the circle.

Shuffle/Stop/Share/Go

I learned this closing activity from a fellow facilitator, Kirsten Nielson, in Madison, WI. It is especially useful for large groups and when there is little time for group discussion. Many variations of this popular activity integrate movement and reflection; see Teachable Moments *(p. 204).*

Facilitation Suggestions:

- Have the group form a circle and, if appropriate, have each participant place one hand on the shoulder of his or her neighbor.

- The group shuffles clockwise until a group member says "stop."

- At that point, the group stops mid-shuffle, and the person who stopped the group shares something positive he or she experienced or observed during the day, and ends by saying "go." The group shuffles in the other direction, and so on.

- This activity is great for kids' groups, in that it negates the need to sit still while listening to others share.

I often use variations of some of my favorite metaphoric activities as a group closing experience. My favorite closing activity engages groups of three or four in creating a drawing that represents the group's experience together. I give them a big piece of paper, colorful fat magic markers, and just 5 or 10 minutes to create a symbol or pictorial representation of the group's experience. Using markers and limiting time keeps the task playful and minimizes concerns about artistic abilities. I then have each group stand up together and present its drawing to the rest of the group. The descriptions are usually humorous, playful, and often quite insightful, and they help end the experience on a positive and memorable note. Artistic methods can be especially powerful as closing activities; I have seen group members spontaneously create songs and poems and raps to describe their experience. This artwork then becomes a memento of the group's experience.

The object or card reflection activities I mentioned previously can be very effective when closing an experience. Have the group members use the objects or cards to tell a story of their experience together. Ask them to come to a consensus and pick three of these

symbols to describe where they were when they arrived, where they "went" as a group, and what is next or what they plan to do with the learning.

Giving participants an opportunity to choose or presenting them with a memento serves as a reminder of the group's and/or their own individual growth, change, achievements, and personal goals solidified through the experience.

Be thoughtful about planning and leaving time for a meaningful closing with your group. The closing moments are your opportunity to help the group pull the experience together and make the learning tangible by helping them articulate their experience so they truly do "take it away" and apply it to future experiences. This can be the time when people come forward and communicate the value of the group experience in a way they haven't before because they see it as their last chance to do so.

For more ideas for group closing activities see *A Teachable Moment* or *Reflective Learning: Theory and Practice* by Deb Sugerman, Kathy Doherty, Mike Gass, and Dan Garvey.

Benefits of Reflective Practice

In American society we don't teach people to be reflective learners. Reflection and time for introspection aren't emphasized in our "just do it" or "get it done" mentality. We are bombarded with information. Children are often hustled through scheduled, 50-minute lesson plans during their school day, and many are overly busy with extra-curricular activities and sports after school along with loads of homework.

People don't often just sit down under a tree and think quietly, journal, or draw. TVs are generally on from the moment people come home from work till they go to bed. In the 21st century we live with lots of background noise. Because many people are not accustomed to reflecting, when they enter a group situation and are asked to reflect, many find it awkward or difficult. Facilitators need to remember that reflection takes practice. Just

"Life is not a problem to be solved, but a reality to be experienced."
Kierkegaard

as we think about sequencing other program activities to match participants' growth and development, we need to think the same way about processing.

I have been fortunate to work with a number of groups over a long period of time. Processing starts to become second nature with these groups where participants are involved in a sequence of reflective activities and build their skills and comfort with the group over time. Ideally groups will get to the point where they spontaneously engage in reflective discussion without prodding from the facilitator. Recently I saw a group of students I have worked with for a few years finish a particularly difficult challenge on the ropes course. When they finished, they immediately gathered into a huddle and started talking excitedly about what had happened. There was no prodding from me or their teachers—we didn't even need to be there. It was encouraging to see how far these group members, who two years prior were very resistant to participating and sharing as a group, had come. Program facilitators can even see that kind of progress in a single day when they carefully sequence a variety of reflective activities throughout the day's events.

Reflection is what ties the experience together. It helps create purpose, meaning, and focus for an activity. The educational philosopher John Dewey stated that people do not truly learn from an experience until they reflect on it and decide how the experience is meaningful and relevant to their lives. Modern-day, brain-based research supports his theory, validating the belief that taking the time for reflection and using a variety of different kinds of reflective techniques facilitate learning. Brain-based research and brain-compatible learning theory suggest that this type of reflection is not just beneficial but necessary to the learning process (Sousa, 2006; Jensen, 2004).

One of the most important benefits of engaging learners in the process of reflection is that it develops insight—a difficult but important life skill to teach and learn. Reflective practice allows individuals to accept responsibility for their learning and apply it to future situations. When participants reflect on their role in an activity, they learn to recognize their skills and strengths by naming them. Through the formal recognition of their skills and strengths they become more aware of their inner resources and more likely to call upon them in future life situations.

Chapter 7

Tying It All Together

What is the value of experiential education?
What did the group learn?
What comes next?
Has the group changed?
Was it worth it?
So what did it all mean?
Did it work?
How do I do better next time?

"The self-reflective practitioner processes information and feedback
gathered from everyday work, continually developing and refining
theories about how and why things 'work' in experiential education."
David Kolb

Throughout this book I emphasize the importance of reflection as
an integral part of experiential education. This is true for facilitators as well as participants. Facilitators who are able to regularly
reflect on their work and its meanings, methods, and outcomes are
able to continually improve their practice by looking more deeply
into the why behind what they do and how it works.

Those who undertake regular reflection and evaluation gather valuable information that improves their program and their skills as a facilitator. Most programs need a way to demonstrate their effectiveness to clients and program funders, so formal evaluation is an ongoing and important part of program development. This research and formal evaluation of programs also helps validate the experiential education field and could be useful in informing and enhancing the work of peers.

Many facilitators don't have much experience with research beyond a college statistics class. Some of us have a resistance to or apprehension about taking on research because we think it emphasizes data and facts over the human experience. We may not think we have the time, resources, or ability to engage in formal evaluation. Research doesn't have to be boring, intimidating, or daunting. There are many ways to gather information about your program and research and evaluate outcomes. A variety of tools are available to practitioners, and many methods combine qualitative and quantitative information to incorporate "the human experience" with specific, measurable outcomes information. Some of my experiences in becoming a more reflective practitioner and my efforts in record keeping and evaluation are shared on the following pages. This includes my experimentation with action research—an innovative approach to outcomes-based evaluation.

Record Keeping

In the last chapter I spoke of the value of keeping a facilitator journal. Facilitators need to think of themselves as participants in the experience, whose reflections are worth noting. Useful daily records might address questions such as:

- What activities did you plan, and then which ones did you and the group actually do?

- How did the group progress through those activities?

- What teachable moments arose?

- Did you learn something new about an activity? Was there a lesson for you as a facilitator?

- Was there an important moment that should be shared with another interested party?

- Did the group meet its goals?

- Based on what happened, do you recommend any specific next steps for the group?

- Did you learn a new trick or tip from a fellow facilitator?

- What went well? What would you do differently next time?

- Are there photos or artwork from the experience that should be shared?

- Did any risk management issues arise that your program needs to examine?

- How are you going to follow up with this group?

Taking time for record keeping can be one of the most challenging aspects of facilitation. As facilitators we spend a great deal of time and energy planning, preparing, and implementing group experiences. Often, when one program ends we move onto the next without much time spent on reflection of program outcomes. I find that after planning, preparing, and "giving my all" during a group session, I feel quite happily exhausted by the effort and ready to take a break. My first inclination and that of many of my fellow facilitators, who work in fast-paced programs, is to breathe a sigh of relief and get ready for the next program or task.

Tips for Facilitator Reflection/Information Gathering

- Do it right after the group. The accuracy of your memory will fade over time. The best time might be the moment the group exits, before you clean up or move out of the program space.

- If you are co-leading, include your co-leader in this reflection. You might have very different perspectives and observations about the group and program.

- Note if you have taken photos or collected any artwork or drawings that could be useful for later evaluation.

- Share activity records with interested parties, such as participants who might use the activities in the future and/or administrators who might want to know what took place.

- Organize any collected data—photos, drawings, quotes, journal statements, evaluation forms, etc.

Practitioners who work in mental health or other treatment settings are usually required to chart individual and group experiences regularly—and there are systems in place to facilitate this process. Those who are not required to do so after every group or don't have systems in place to help ease this process can miss out on important reflection and opportunities for improving the quality of their programs.

Some facilitators keep journals or activity log books. A record of successful sequences of activities can be very useful in planning future programming, both for you as facilitator and for others who might work with the same or similar groups. For ongoing groups a log book designed for that specific group can help you see their progress over time, plan the next steps, and evaluate areas in which you might want to focus more attention or look for help. It can also be a source of valuable data in grant writing and formal evaluation for funding agencies and policy makers.

Record keeping became invaluable in my long-term work with local schools where I interacted with 20 or more teachers and their classrooms year after year. I needed a way to keep track of the activities I facilitated class to class. This forced me to keep a more detailed record, motivating me to create a log book for recording information about specific class groups, program goals, activities presented, and outcomes (see Figure 10.1). It has been well worth the effort, as I used it in writing curriculum and planning lessons. It has also been a tool for exploring ways to connect these community building activities to academic content such as math and science lessons as well as team building.

Community Building Activity Log

Date: _____   School/Site: _____

Facilitators: _____   Classroom: _____

Group Name: _____(attach student roster if applicable)

Number Served: Students: _____   Teachers: _____

Goals for the Group: _____

_____

_____

Activities Planned: _____

_____

_____

Activities Completed: _____

_____

Outcomes: _____

_____

Facilitator Notes: _____

_____

_____

Next Steps/Follow Up: _____

_____

Data: _____

Photos: _____   Artwork: _____   Reflection: _____

Figure 10.1 Community Building Activity Log
© Jennifer Stanchfield/Wood 'N' Barnes Publishing, Tips & Tools, 2007.

The logs serve as a tool for communication with fellow staff who co-lead the programs. They are tools for the teachers and student peer mentors to use as examples of activity sequences they could use with other groups or in future years. The logs are useful when I develop and facilitate a similar program with another school. And they can also be used as part of a formal evaluation of the outcomes of the program over the long term.

Did It Work?: Outcomes-Based Evaluation

As thoughtful facilitators we want to identify whether our program has impacted, benefited, or changed our participants, and if so, how. In what ways were they impacted? What did they learn? How have they changed? What was it about the activities or specific methods or aspects of group work that impacted them?

Trying to find the answers to these questions is part of ongoing program improvement and refinement. It also is a requirement in many programs. We live in a results-driven society, and many of our programs are grant funded, so we have to find ways to demonstrate outcomes. Doing so can take the form of questionnaires, surveys, or interviews. Evaluation can be done internally or through professional, outside program evaluators. An evaluation process varies depending on a variety of factors:

- What kind of program you are working with?

- What do you want to find out about your program?

- Are you evaluating individual outcomes of participants or group progress?

- Who needs to see the results of your evaluation?

Some of the best evaluation processes I have seen use a variety of methods, both quantitative and qualitative. These could include a combination of a formal research instrument and outside researcher along with case studies and testimonials gathered internally from participants. Facilitators can find resources for program evaluation and ways to track individual progress that are specific to the type of facilitation they do through professional organizations in their field. Mental health agencies have "quality assurance" programs with models for evaluating outcomes. For facilitators looking to evaluate their programs, a list of resources is provided in Appendix A.

One of the approaches to research and evaluation that I found most valuable in my own practice is action research—an experiential approach to evaluation that I discovered during my graduate work and my time working in a number of public schools in Wisconsin.

Action Research

Action research is a practitioner-as-researcher approach where professionals actively take part in a structured inquiry and reflection into their own work in order to identify how to better impact their clients. Practitioners engage in action research with the intent that the research will inform and change their future practices. It is carried out in the context of the work/learning environment where action takes place and addresses the immediate and relevant questions that practitioners face day to day as they strive to improve their work. It is a cycle of posing questions, gathering data, reflecting and sharing with others, and identifying next steps. Groups of practitioners may collaborate on studying an issue, topic, or question. The collaboration improves communication between educators and helps broaden perspectives.

Action research, which has its roots in the philosophy of experiential education, encourages practitioners to act as "collaborative researchers" with their students/clients to create a record of experience and share outcomes with other practitioners. Action research is based on the philosophy that practitioners are in a great place to actively study their work and share this information with others in their field. Practitioners have a great deal to learn through actively reflecting on their own practice and finding ways to share and collaborate with their colleagues and other interested parties. Just like the work we do in experiential education with our clients, the process of understanding and improving one's work starts from reflecting on one's own experience.

The action research movement is well established throughout England, where it is used by educators, health professionals, police departments, and corporate programs. It has become more widely spread in public school systems and community organizations in the United States over the past decade as a form of staff development.

As a model for staff development it motivates educators by giving them an active role in identifying the purposes and ends of their work. Rather than just getting educators to comply with solutions and expert knowledge from outside, they are involved in recognizing the wealth of expertise and knowledge that they have to offer each other. This insider knowledge is what Donald Schon in his book *The Reflective Practitioner* (1983) called "knowledge in action."

The Madison, Wisconsin Public School District was one of the first U.S. school districts to implement action research as a form of ongoing staff development. They have created a number of action research groups where school professionals are given an opportunity to gain graduate or advancement credit by participating in research groups. These teachers are given release time to meet monthly, brainstorm, and support each other in researching

"The real voyage of discovery consists not in seeing new landscapes but in having new eyes." Proust

what is happening in their classrooms.* This is an example of what many call "collaborative action research."

Although the educators are studying different issues in their various schools and classrooms, they all come together regularly to share ideas about how they are gathering information and how it is going to be shared and acted upon. For example, one teacher might be trying to evaluate the success of a new curriculum, another some behavioral management techniques in their classroom, and another the needs for the special education program. Alternative forms of gathering and sharing evaluative information, such as combining interviews, qualitative surveys, and analysis of students' artwork and reflection, are encouraged in these action research groups. I was able to participate in some of the Madison School District's Experiential Education Action Research cohort group's meetings and activities as part of my coursework. It inspired me to focus my efforts on researching my work with the Middleton School District challenge course class.

A Personal Account of Action Research

In 1998, I was fortunate enough to be involved in the development of an extensive experiential education program at Stevens Point School District in Stevens Point, WI. My experiences there inspired me to continue and expand my work in the public schools. While completing my graduate studies at Minnesota State University–Mankato's graduate program in experiential education, I started working as a consultant developing experiential curriculum with teachers in a variety of Wisconsin Public Schools. A research course requirement was part of my graduate degree. I was intrigued by what I was hearing from a few teachers about something called action research and found that there was a graduate course

---

* For more information on Madison's Action Research program visit www. madisonk12.wi.us/sod/car—a comprehensive Web site about action research methods and guidelines for data gathering and reporting.

on action research being offered by Ken Zeichner, Ph.D. at the University of Wisconsin–Madison.

When I chose to register for that class, I was coteaching a semester-long physical education course at Middleton High School in Middleton, WI and working on my graduate thesis project. All of these elements came together, and I embarked on a practitioner reflection project that enhanced my career in a way no formal training ever has.

I was hired at Middleton as a consultant, helping teachers, counselors, and other school professionals use experiential education methods in grades K-12 as part of counseling and prevention, character education, and physical/health education programs. One of the most rewarding aspects of that experience was coteaching the high school physical education program's Ropes Challenge Class with Donna Richter.

Planning our first quarter, Donna and I recognized the challenge of balancing time for activities and reflection in the limited time given for physical education class. We were inspired to experiment with journaling as part of the student's course requirements by a couple of factors. First, the school district had a writing requirement for physical education that had previously involved pop quizzes. Donna had never been thrilled about administering these, so she was open to experimenting with a more interesting and effective way to integrate writing into physical education class. Second, I had recently attended an impressive workshop by Camille Bunting, Ph.D. of Texas A&M, who shared about an interesting research project involving the use of journaling as part of a semester-long challenge course class she had recently taught. She and her graduate student researchers had divided the students' statements into a model showing the phases of group development, demonstrating the value of the challenge course in positive group development.

Donna and I agreed that journaling seemed to be a worthwhile experiment for our students. We were not disappointed. Never before had I received such detailed, meaningful insights and feedback from participants about what they were gaining from their experience. As students shared their class journals, we were able to learn from their perspectives what was happening in the process of group development and individual learning.

We observed throughout the semester how the students were changing and growing together. It was incredibly rewarding as an educator to see positive outcomes and the value of the work we do. Despite some grumbling about journaling during the semester, at the end of the course students shared that they were pleased to have a memento of their experience. We observed that their personal insight and writing skills improved greatly throughout the semester. We were helping them develop a lifelong reflective skill.

The students' journal analysis became one of the most useful tools for evaluating the effectiveness of our course and became an integral piece of my action research project. It turned out to be an essential part of our program, giving us valuable perspectives on experiential education as a modality and which methods and activities were most effective with our students.

With the students' permission we read and transcribed their journals. I divided all of the entries by class session and then sorted the entries by the different domains covered in the Wisconsin standards for physical education, specific school and program goals, and the personal goals and objectives students had initially identified for participation in the course.

We ended up using the material gathered from these student journals to look at ways to improve the course and change our lesson plans and curriculum for the next semester. The most significant result of the journal analysis was that the student testimonials demonstrated the value of experiential methods and the challenge course program and how the program activities and outcomes connect to specific academic standards. This information was passed on to school administrators and grant funders, enabling teachers to continue to expand and fund the school's adventure program. I find the students' journaling statements valuable to this day when sharing information about the possibilities of experiential programming and to paint a picture of how the process of group building works.

Action researchers are encouraged to use a variety of methods of gathering data. Along with the journal analysis, I made an audio documentary of the challenge course class and a photo journal. I also engaged an outside observer to come in and observe and interview students in the class. The information I gathered helped Donna and me answer many important questions about our methods. I focused on the following questions as part of my action research project:

1) Can experiential-based, group problem-solving and adventure activities build a classroom community, increasing a supportive, cohesive, emotionally safe school environment?

2) Can adventure activities improve self-esteem?

3) Should students be taught to belay? What is the value? Is it safe practice?

4) Is experiential-based adventure education an effective method for meeting the Wisconsin Model Academic Standards for Physical Education?

Student Testimonials as Action Research Data

The following excerpts from students' journals and end-of-the-year evaluations speak to the questions I researched in my action research project. For more data on the questions see Appendix B.

1) Can experiential-based, group problem-solving and adventure activities build a classroom community, increasing a supportive, cohesive, emotionally safe school environment?

Journal excerpts:

"I am getting to know people better and I can actually say hi to them when before I didn't have a clue who they were. And there is meaning behind the hello instead of a hello that means absolutely nothing."

"Nick and I were practicing tying knots today and joking around. I really like that aspect of this class. I didn't really know Nick before this class; now I guess we've struck up a bit of a friendship. I am starting to feel that about other people in this class who I didn't know or actually thought I didn't like before now. We really have a bond that allows us to laugh and play, work and think together."

"Sometimes it is really challenging working in a group. I usually don't have to rely on other people to get things done, but this class is forcing me to work on that."

"I was actually getting into the challenge by taking some initiative with helping spotting and lifting people through the web. We really got a chance to take some serious responsibility in this activity to keep everyone safe. I feel like I am gaining a strong sense of trust with the entire class."

"We worked together and we were better at considering everyone's suggestions. We were supportive of each other and kind and made sure everyone felt included."

"I thought the Have You Ever? game helped us to become more familiar with unusual things about our classmates. I think it is a good exercise because it helped us appreciate how we are all from different backgrounds, yet still have a lot in common."

"I've learned how I react and interact with others, and how I can be more patient and more understanding of others."

End-of-the-year evaluations:

> "I really enjoyed being around so many different kinds of people. Their attitudes and support for others helped me get through many of the challenges, and they made me feel comfortable with it. Otherwise I don't think that I would have ever met and talked to most of the people in the class, let alone trusted them with my life as I did with belaying."

> "Our class as a group has changed dramatically. At first no one felt comfortable working together. By the end, we had pulled together as one problem-solving unit."

> "The 'challenge by choice' policy gave me a sense of freedom."

> "This class really focuses on group effort. I've never felt so close to my peers in any other class—it helps the way I feel about coming to school each day."

> "I liked how I started to feel very comfortable in this class; I got to know everyone well, and when we created the full-value agreement I trusted they wouldn't judge me, so I could relax and be myself."

2) Can adventure activities improve self-esteem?

Journal excerpts:

> "I really felt good after I saved Rebecca from falling into the piranha filled waters. It sort of felt like I had done something beneficial for the group. I felt like I had saved us from disaster."

> "Sam and I really stepped up as leaders at the start. It leads me to think of myself as more of a leader. Maybe I have always been that way but haven't noticed it till now. That's pretty cool."

> "I am using these challenges to push my comfort zone. Last class I not only exceeded my expectations, but those of my peers. When

I was the last one left in the balloon game I was surprised. Frankly I expected to be out within the first few minutes. I am seeing my abilities differently in this class. I have not thought of myself as skilled or athletic or strong. When I climbed the activity that those other stronger people had trouble with and felt an unexpected steadiness I became more confident; many people were surprised, that someone not tall was so successful. I realize some of my past experience in gymnastics helped as well as my persistence and attitude. I am feeling a sense of satisfaction with myself."

"It felt good when everyone used my idea to solve the planet game. I wasn't going to speak up at first but I did—and it was worth it! "

"I breezed right through all the knot tying and belay preparation. I guess a lot of observation can pay off. It made me feel good that I seemed to catch on so fast. Now I am the knot teacher. I like being able to help others; it feels good to have something to offer them. I had never seen myself as a leader before but that is changing."

End-of-the-year evaluations:

"I feel more confident in my abilities."

"I liked how good I felt about myself after doing challenges."

"I think I have grown as a person."

"I am more social, accepting, and happy."

"I have become more adventuresome."

"I am more aware of my own fears and how to approach them."

3) Should students be taught to belay? What is the value? Is it safe practice?

Journal excerpts:

"Wow! Today was very scary, yet exciting. I never thought that I would be able to belay

anyone. But I did it! Somehow I managed the strength and power and confidence in myself to do it. I was nervous, I thought about woosing out, but this voice inside me told me to push on. And sure enough I did it. I belayed someone successfully. I am very glad I had the opportunity to take this class. All the things, especially belaying, have taught me what I can do and how I rely on others and that I can be a person that they can rely on."

"I have been watching how seriously people take belaying. Those who usually joke around are really focused, kind of nervous because they realize this is a big deal, so they are really paying attention. I think we are actually learning more from the belaying than the

climbing, at least about being responsible, focused, and confident."

"Belaying teaches you patience, coordination, and trust. You really have to be confident to allow someone to place a ton of trust and confidence in you. The whole thing with belaying and climbing is to learn to trust others and to lean on them for support instead of trying to do everything yourself. I trusted Joe to belay me because he showed me he was ready. I am confident in taking the responsibility myself, especially having a partner as a back-up belayer so we can work together."

"The belayers were able to talk and have a good time, but when the climb started, everyone got more serious and focused on taking care of their climber."

End-of-the-year evaluations:

"Belaying each other made me trust my classmates and was fundamental in our group building. It's an essential part of the whole class. If only teachers belayed, it would be an individual class as opposed to a group experience."

"I think that if we didn't learn to belay, then we wouldn't have gotten so far and we wouldn't have learned the responsibility of taking care of someone else on the belay system. The value of learning how to belay is that it is a skill that takes your mind and body's full concentration. And it's fun."

"It lets us take control of the situation and depend on ourselves."

"We use gratitude, honesty, and trust when we belay."

"People should see how responsible and careful we are when we belay."

4) Is experiential-based adventure education an effective method for meeting the Wisconsin Standards for Physical Education?

Journal excerpts:

"I am not really sure why I see climbing as way for creative expression, but I guess I feel this way because there is no one right way to do it and it requires a lot of careful planning. Even though I was going pretty fast trying to cross the wall, I now see more that you have to take your time as you climb because if you don't there probably won't be that much of a growth in one's individual skill for climbing. It seems that as a class we will be able to improve steadily as a group because we all do a good job spotting and being able to trust one another, which is important for many reasons."

"Wow! I just climbed the wall, and for me, it was really exciting. I didn't have many worries or fears—well actually I did. I was really nervous. Just the fear of falling I guess. It is a lot harder than it looks. Your forearms get all tense and hot. It feels so good to have accomplished that finally."

"All of these activities have helped me practice staying calm and thinking before I act."

"We could choose to go across the wall blindfolded. This is easy to relate to real life. Sometimes you have to accomplish a task without knowing where to go or what to do next. You depend on others to give you advice and lead you. This is important because sometimes you have to recognize when you need help and that need is okay."

End-of-the-year evaluations:

"I liked the climbing challenges and making my body do things it wasn't before."

"I have become a stronger, more active person—the physical climbing activities became easier each time I tried them."

"I gained new perspectives on solving problems by listening to what others had to say, and I learned a lot about new methods of thinking things through."

"I think I have gained insight on how to be a much better listener as well as a better communicator while taking this class."

"This filled my gym requirement in a more meaningful and memorable way—this class has some actual application to real life in terms of the team building you gain unlike regular gym class."

The Impact of the Action Research Experience

As you can see, taking part in an action research project helped me solidify my own personal theory and approach to experiential facilitation. It helped me understand why I intuitively and repeatedly use some of the activities and approaches that I do. It helped me step back and look at what participants were learning and understand the building blocks of this process.

The insights were invaluable in my curriculum writing project for Middleton High School and have influenced many projects since then. Donna and I used the information from the journal entries, journal surveys, student interviews, and student feedback questionnaire to design a better class for the next semester. We changed up the sequence of some of our activities, added some new activities, let go of some that we had previously thought were important, and adjusted the journaling assignment a great deal. We passed on what we had learned to our colleague who was teaching the other section of this class, influencing changes in his lesson plans as well as ours. The information sparked the idea for us to create a "teaching assistant" position for seniors who had taken the class the first semester to help teach the next semester's class. This eventually morphed into a peer leadership project that involved these students' sharing what they had learned in the primary grades. We shared the information through staff development workshops with other teachers in the district the following year. Most significantly, we used the data to demonstrate outcomes in a grant proposal and received additional funding to continue the program.

Over the years I have continued to use qualitative surveys to learn about participants' reactions to experience. I have collected meaningful testimonials from the participant questionnaires about how experiential group work has impacted them. The testimonials have helped me better articulate the practice of experiential education, identify areas to focus on in future programs and what areas to change. The following pages show some example questionnaires and the testimonials gathered.

End-of-Year Student Evaluation
Ropes Challenge Course Class

Think back to the beginning of the year. You were asked to set goals for the year in your initial journal assignment. Did you reach any of these goals? If so, how?

What did you like about this class?

Are there moments that stand out for you?

Do you feel you have changed over the semester?

Do you feel our class as a group has changed?

Have you done anything in this class that you thought you would never do?

Imagine your school district came to a funding crisis; the adventure program was one of the items proposed to be cut. If you were interviewed by a school board member about whether they should keep the challenge course, what arguments would you make for its value?

What other suggestions do you have for us about the class for next year?

What did you think of the full-value agreement process?

Which activities that you participated in this semester were your favorites; which were your least favorite? Please be specific; which of the games did you like? Which low elements did you like?

There are people who don't believe students should be allowed to belay; what do you think about that? How would you respond to that?

Peer Leadership Institute Questionnaire

1. In what way did this experience help you grow as a person?

2. What feelings did you take away from your time in the leadership institute?

3. Give an example of a time that you took a leadership role during the week.

4. We had financial support to make this program happen. What would you say to the program sponsors about the value of the program?

PEP Grant Teacher Survey

Have you used any of the adventure activities, techniques, or ideas you learned through your trainings with your students? If so, how often/how many?

Did you experience success with these activities? Comments?

Have you noticed any changes in your teaching since training began?

Have you noticed any changes in your students since implementing these activities?

If your school district proposed to cut funding for adventure programming and they asked you to make an argument for the value of this project, what would you say?

Student Questions Sampler

What were some high points for you this year?
What activities do you remember most?

Did you find yourself taking part in an activity or challenge
that you never imagined you would? If so, explain.

Which activity or experience taught you the most? Explain.

What changes have you seen in
yourself and your peers from 8th to 11th grade? Do you think our
program helped with those changes? Explain.

_____

_____

_____

_____

_____

Student Questions Sampler (cont.)

> How would you describe your experience on the challenge course? What feeling did you take away from the experience?

What arguments would you make to a leader in your school for what makes this program valuable or worthwhile?

_____

_____

_____

_____

_____

_____

Some challenge course programs don't allow students to belay. What are some of the values for allowing students to belay?

Would you be interested in being a part of future programs and learning how to become a peer mentor?

The following question about school board funding garnered the most insightful comments from participants at Middleton High School. I continue to include this question in my surveys and find the answers incredibly moving, inspiring me to continue this kind of work! The following student responses paint a picture of the value of challenge course programming in their school:

Question: The board of education is considering whether or not to fund the challenge course program next year. What arguments would you make for or against their choosing to fund the program?

"I am a Harding High School student who hopes that the Board of Education can continue the funding of the adventure program. Some of my reasons are, you get to experience new things, you can learn from it, and you can have fun. This has been a great thing for me. I learned to trust others and others trust in me. Next, if you keep funding this, more students will get the opportunity to learn these things that other schools don't have. I learned how to belay and enjoy myself. I learned about my classmates. We get challenged by this adventure program which shows the other sides of us. Without it school would be boring."

"I have taken the Adventure Program for two years now. I met different people, participated in many different activities, and learned a lot. It improves a lot of skills we are going to use in later times of our lives: communicating skills, problem-solving and responsibility skills. We listened to each other, gave ideas to our peers verbally and non-verbally. We also used problem-solving skills to get over hard obstacles. We took responsibility of our actions because we knew what was the right thing to do. This class was a means to improve self-confidence, esteem, and commitment. I personally felt a lot better and determined when I almost got the top end of

a challenge and succeeded with the help of my peers and teachers. Finally, we just had fun. It was a new challenge every day, and everybody was always excited to try it. Most people participated, and helped each other. On the first day of a new challenge, everybody would gather around to support the first climber, and see what they would have to face. I also noticed that even those students that didn't complete a challenge would always say 'at least I got up there and tried.'"

"The Adventure Program is very important to the well-being of the students. This is true in many aspects of our lives because we go around school with one group of friends and don't give other people a chance because most of us lack self-confidence and through the Adventure Program we were and are able to have many people from different backgrounds and cliques and bring them together in an area outside peer pressure and teach them to communicate and be confident and it is a very successful program."

Teacher Survey Responses

Inspired by what I learned from student responses during my action research project, I wanted to gather information from teachers who were being trained in using experiential methods. We asked for feedback from teachers in Bridgeport, CT about their experiences with implementing these kinds of activities with their classes. We surveyed them a few times through the first year of training from us. The first survey was given about three months into their training and included the following questions:

- Did you experience success with these activities? Comments?

- Have you noticed any changes in your teaching since your training began?

- Have you noticed any changes in your students since implementing these activities?

Here are some teachers' responses to the Bridgeport PEP Grant January Teacher Survey:

Did you experience success with these activities? Comments?

"The kids especially loved the problems of the rope. I actually had one class solve all three problems in two sessions."

"Most have been fairly successful—only problems are getting along in groups and letting all members contribute to the group instead of a couple dominating."

"There is more participation, but there are still up and down days."

"Some activities have needed to be modified."

"It was amazing to me to watch the classes try to solve the activities and get along doing it. The enthusiasm was great, and now I have classes asking to do the activities again."

"Some classes had difficulty with rules—it took two classes for them to figure out how to play."

"Some were more successful than others, but all were enjoyable."

"One class really liked the nonverbal activities. The kids like the change, they liked team choosing."

"I felt good that they were getting the concepts of team work, trust, cooperative problem-solving."

"Many activities were successful, others were horrible—but they learned firsthand that if they don't cooperate, the 'challenge' will fail. It is difficult for me to watch it fail but I realize it's part of the process."

"I have witnessed more participation, improved cooperation amongst classmates, more class enthusiasm, students taking on leadership roles (usually the typically difficult students), and better behavior."

Have you noticed any changes in your teaching since your training began?

"I require student feedback more, less instruction, more open-ended directions, more observation of my students."

"I'm starting to understand the value of these activities and how success relates to taking the time to do the group norms agreements."

"I have the students think more and struggle a bit rather than just giving them the answer."

"Less yelling—finding that I have to be a little more patient and less anxious."

"My knowledge of these activities has increased, which has given me more confidence to teach this to the kids. Before I was afraid and a little pessimistic about it. I didn't think these city kids would go for adventure, but I was wrong."

"I am able to facilitate better and teach less. It was highly frustrating at the beginning, and I found myself stepping in to correct inappropriate behavior. I am more able to allow them to work through this now."

"I am more patient. I also feel a sense of worth and accomplishment. I feel there is more value to my field of occupation."

"I feel more relaxed and alive. I have new activities to try."

"We all seem to have a more of a 'team' mentality. I tend to stress competition less and cooperation more."

Have you noticed any changes in your students since implementing these activities?

"I've seen shy kids come out of their shell, followers become leaders, and quiet kids become enthusiastic and excited."

"YES! They are better behaved."

"They are excited about the program and are always asking, 'What are we going to do today?' or they want to repeat an activity."

"They are starting to realize that arguing and putting down is counterproductive to this curriculum and life in general."

"Overall much more cooperation during activities."

"They are definitely more attuned to listening and working together better. They still have a long way to go, however."

The second survey was taken about 6 months into their training and program implementation. The information helped us understand the impact of our training on teachers and how the activities were being used with their students. One significant aspect was that teachers' self-esteem and self-perception seemed to be as positively affected by the experience as the students'. The questions on this survey included:

- When using adventure activities in your classroom, what moments stand out for you?

- What specific changes have you seen in your classroom?

- Do you think there is any change in the way students perceive themselves? If so, how?

- Do you have any information about what is happening in your classroom that you would like to share?

- Are there some new techniques or activity variations that you have had success with? If so, what?

- How do you see yourself implementing these activities for the remainder of this year? What are your goals with using Adventure Education, and how do you see it fitting into the next school year?

- Comment on your training. What have you liked? What suggestions do you have for us?

Excerpts from the Bridgeport PEP Grant March Teacher Survey:

When using adventure activities in your classroom, what moments stand out for you?

"When students that don't usually participate get involved in activities. When a student who is usually a pain becomes a leader (this happens often)."

"It's refreshing to see 50 kids in a gym working together with limited teacher interaction."

"When students say they cannot do it, and then are able to complete the task."

"When someone chooses to be a partner with that one student no one wants to be with."

What specific changes have you seen in your classroom?

"More communication, less tolerant of other kids acting out, more positive peer role modeling, and self-correcting behaviors."

"The students are definitely beginning to problem-solve better and especially listen to each other better during the process."

"They are accepting more responsibility for each other."

"Students starting to huddle up and implement a new plan."

"Students thinking before they act."

"I don't have to explain or mediate as often."

"All the kids want to play, not just the athletes. Kids who usually don't participate are participating."

"Classes that were having difficulty working together in groups and getting along improved after using these activities just a few times."

Do you think there is any change in the way students perceive themselves? If so, how?

"Yes, the shy kids seem to be more comfortable."

"Many students feel better about themselves, and have a better understanding of peers."

"I've seen a very distinct change in regards to their ability to talk, share, and take charge. Others are participating in trust activities who were once afraid."

"Students who probably would not participate much find things that are either challenging to them or easy for them to do."

Do you have any information about what is happening in your classroom that you would like to share?

"The Us/Not Us list was useful, and it worked. The Were We Successful? reflections were useful, and I will use again."

"I have had students come back and say that they have talked with their parents about some of the activities."

"I have been taking photos of the students in several activities (varied ages). I am using the journal. It helps me see what is working and how the kids are changing."

"I have been using journals with all the 45+ participating students. I would like to begin taking pictures and placing them in a collage. Some of the quotes from the journals that I recall are: "I hated PE but this stuff I love, I hope we never play basketball again!" and "I didn't used to trust, but now I am starting to."

"We have a 5ᵗʰ grade teacher who has a very difficult class. Since we implemented the adventure education strategies with them she has learned to have more control of her classroom."

Are there some new techniques or activity variations that you have had success with? If so, what?

"I've enjoyed using innovative techniques for team choosing that Jen gave us (partner dividing). My kids have enjoyed group juggling and Have You Ever?"

"One technique I have used to encourage the students to work together more is to explain what I am as a facilitator and then let them know that they are now the teachers."

"In the river crossing we have adjusted the distances to accommodate our younger classes."

How do you see yourself implementing these activities for the remainder of this year? What are your goals with using adventure education, and how do you see it fitting into the next school year?

"For the remainder of the year I want students to continue to improve on trust activities and initiatives. Next year, I plan to start in September and work all year with one or two specific classes at least once a week so that we can experience the outdoor course at Wilbur Cross and all of the high level activities in our gym."

"I will keep conducting all of these games and activities so that I can build on what the students already know and have participated in next year."

"I have been using one class as a pilot group to implement various activities. Most of my other classes have only been able to participate in two or three games. Next year I will commit to using this approach in all of my classes."

Comment on your training. What have you liked? What suggestions do you have for us?

"I have enjoyed the light spiritedness and the obvious progressions."

"The training has been extremely professional, well organized, and sequential."

"I feel confident as I begin to teach and facilitate. Watching you as we went through the activities helped me to learn facilitating. The amount of material available to us at times was overwhelming, but I know that will improve with time. I hope training and workshops are available next year to provide needed continuity and support."

"There are some classes that still haven't bought into the trust and cooperation needed, but most have and I have been pleased. It's fun, exciting and great to work closely with other colleagues that I never even knew before."

"Being a first year teacher these activities helped me get to know other teachers. I hope these games will welcome in new students."

I hope that sharing my experiences with research and program information will inspire others to become reflective practitioners and make research part of their regular practice. Regardless of the specific methods you utilize, research is accessible even to those of us not professionally trained in research and statistics. Evaluation of program curriculum, activities, methods and participant outcomes is integral to quality, effective, sustainable facilitation. Collaborating with participants and other facilitators in systematic reflection can be an incredibly rewarding experience for all involved.

Closing Thoughts

"Take the first step in faith. You don't have to see the whole staircase, just take the first step." Martin Luther King, Jr.

"We can do no great things; only small things with great love." Mother Teresa

Facilitation is an art, rather than a science. By its very nature it is an experiential practice. There is no proven way to best facilitate, no magic bullet, no specific style that works for every group. It takes practice balanced with reflection and more practice. It is a blend of creativity, intuition, experience, flexibility, exploration, and group chemistry. It is an ever-dynamic process of give and take, learning, and development.

The more facilitators take time to think about their practice and collaborate with others, the better they become. The more they participate in reflection on their practice, the further they can go in developing effective techniques. Eventually, facilitators become adept at intuitively reading a group and can easily reach into repertoire for a specific activity or technique. Good facilitators never stop learning.

Having a sense of passion for one's work and a participant-centered approach are essentials to the art of facilitation. Flexibility and creativity combined with careful preparation and a willingness to change the plan when needed are the basis of good practice in facilitation. A sense of fun and the ability not to take one's self too seriously might be most important of all!

Appendix A: Resources for Program Evaluation

Web Resources for Program Evaluation and Research:

www.surveymonkey.com
This Web site offers software to create customized, professional online surveys for your program. This is a very affordable, user-friendly resource for data collection, analysis, and dissemination of information.

www.managementhelp.org
This comprehensive Web site caters to non-profit organizations with free materials and information regarding many issues of program management, including outcomes evaluation. It has many useful links to evaluation tools and resources.

www.uwex.edu/ces/pdande/index/html
Program Logic Model: This model framework for evaluating educational programs was developed by the University of Wisconsin Extension. It could be useful to many programs and practitioners. It has been adopted by the Kellogg Foundation and other universities and grant-funded programs. The Program Logic Model is an ongoing, systematic process to follow when planning, implementing, and evaluating educational programs. The process can be applied on a small scale to an individual workshop, on a larger scale to a comprehensive community initiative, or to a county or statewide program of action.

http://www.wilderdom.com/leg.html
The Life Effectiveness Questionnaire (LEQ) is an excellent tool for monitoring program effectiveness. The LEQ was developed by Garry Richards' staff at Outward Bound Australia in conjunction with James Neill. The LEQ can be used to research and evaluate the outcomes of programs that aim to enhance students' personal and social development. Many programs use it for investigating effective personal and behavioral change in outdoor education programs, and it can be customized to measure specific, targeted program goals.

http://www.wilderdom.com/research.php
Web site created by an author of the Life Effectiveness Questionnaire research instrument. Valuable information on experiential education and researching your program.

http://cart.rmcdenver.com
C.A.R.T.: Compendium of Assessment and Research Tools for measuring Education and Youth Development Outcomes. The Compendium

of Assessment and Research Tools (CART) is a database that provides information on instruments that measure attributes associated with youth development programs. CART includes descriptions of research instruments, tools, rubrics, and guides and is intended to assist those who have an interest in studying the effectiveness of service-learning, safe and drug-free schools and communities, and other school-based youth development activities.

Articles and Books on Program Evaluation:

Kolb, D. (1991, May). Meaningful Methods: Evaluation without the Crunch. *The Journal of Experiential Education, 14* (1).

Neill, J. T., Marsh, H. W., & Richards, G. E. (1997). *Development and Psychometrics of the Life Effectiveness Questionnaire.* Sydney: University of Western Sydney.

Individual Assessment:

A number of informative articles on student assessment tools regularly appear in the Journal of Physical Education Recreation and Dance. Here are a few that have interesting case studies and specific examples of assessment tools used by educators:

Hensley, L. D. (1997, Sept.). Alternative assessment for physical education. *JOPERD*, pp. 19-24.

Welk, G. & Wook K. (2000, January). Physical activity assessments in physical education: A practical review of instruments and their use in curriculum. *JOPERD, 71(1).*

Worrel, V., Evands-Fletcher, C., & Kovar, S. (2002, September). Assessing the cognitive and affective progress of children. *JOPERD*, pp. 29-34.

Web Site Resources for Action Research:

http://www.madisonk12.wi.us/sod/car/carhomepage.html
Madison Wisconsin Metropolitan School District Classroom Action Research Program Web site. This is a comprehensive, user-friendly website describing Madison's ongoing action research programs. The Web site's most impressive feature is the guidelines for practitioner research and the final report on the nature and impact of action research in the public schools by Dr. Ken Zeichner and Cathy Caro-Bruce.

http://www.bath.ac.uk/~edsajw/
The Bath University Group
Comprehensive Web site on the history and application of action research with links to specific examples and practitioner research projects.

http://www.did.stu.mmu.ac.uk/carn/
Collaborative Action Research Network (CARN) (UK)
The CARN Web site is sponsored by the Center for Applied Research in Education at the University of East Anglia. The CARN group has a broad scope; topics span nursing, teacher education, social work, and business training. Along with contributors from the academic world, members include police officers, school administrators, and classroom teachers.

http://www.alliance.brown.edu/pubs/themes_ed/act_research.pdf
This Web site of the Education Alliance and the Northeast and Islands Regional Education Laboratory includes a booklet on Action Research by Eileen Ferrance and offers links to action research Web sites.

Action Research Books:

Anderson, G., Herr, K., & Nihlen, A. (1994). *Studying your own school: An educator's guide to Qualitative Practitioner Research*. Thousand Oaks, CA: Corwin Press.

Elliot, J. (1991). *Action research for educational change*. Bristol, PA: Open University Press.

Fishman, S. & McCarthy, L. (2000). *Unplayed tapes: A personal history of collaborative teacher research*. New York: Teachers College Press.

Henderson, J. (1992). *Reflective teaching: Becoming an inquiring educator*. New York: Macmillan

Henderson, K., & Bialeschki, M. (2002) Evaluating leisure services: Making enlightened decisions. State College, PA: Venture Publishing.

Hubbard, R.S. & Power, B. M. (1993). *The art of classroom inquiry*. Portsmouth, NH: Heinemann.

Jarvis, P. (1999). *The practitioner-researcher: Developing theory from practice*. San Francisico: Jossey-Bass.

McNiff, J. (1993). *Teaching as learning: An action research approach*. London: Rutledge.

Zeichner, K. & Liston, D. (1996). *Reflective teaching: An introduction*. Mahwah, NJ: Lawrence Erlbaum.

Appendix B: Excerpts From Action Research Project

May, 2001

My evaluation of the curriculum, methods, and outcomes of our Middleton High School's adventure education course using action research consisted of gathering methods in a variety of ways. Our class is so dynamic in nature; it made sense to use a variety of methods to capture the different levels of experience in an adventure education course. The idea for trying to capture the experience of challenge courses on audio and video had been on my mind some time. Getting the opportunity to teach my own class for an entire semester enabled much more experimentation. Initially the journal assignments, audio recordings, etc. were not formally part of action research. I think I was actually setting up an action research project intuitively before I was exposed to the concept through our course.

The journal assignments we gave the students at the beginning of the semester were intended to provide them with an opportunity to develop personal insight, reflection skills, and critical problem-solving skills. They were intended as a form of processing the experience. Many in the field of experiential education adopted John Dewey's idea that in order to truly learn from an experience, there must be time for reflection. In my own philosophy of experiential education this is a significant area I emphasize with my students. Due to limited class time, processing as a group after an experience is often difficult. The journals seemed like a great way to help ensure that this kind of reflection was happening. They not only served that purpose, but also became an extremely valuable tool for Donna Richter and me to evaluate the outcomes of our course and the most effective methods.

The students demonstrated a progression in the group development process through their journal entries. They demonstrated increased insight and improved writing skills. Many describe an increase in self-esteem throughout the semester. All of the students documented an increase in the cohesiveness and communication skills of their class as a whole. The journal entries make very powerful statements about the positive impact of experiential-based adventure education.

The audio recordings process was inspired by my experiences listening to the audio documentary show *This American Life* on National Public Radio. I had noticed in listening to that program that audio recordings capture material that we don't often catch while we are in a situation ourselves or watching it on video. This stood out for me when I started editing the audio recordings of our class sessions. The audio caught layers of the experience I was not aware of, like side comments from the students, details of the students' thinking through problems, and how powerful encouraging words and applause can be.

The interview and video recordings by an outside observer (Catherine Coberly, a teacher from a different school district with no previous experience in adventure education) were another powerful source of information—first in demonstrating in such a positive way how much students gained from the class experience, and also by getting detailed feedback about the sequencing of the curriculum and the success and usefulness of the journaling assignment. It helped us decide which activities to keep in our lesson plans, which ones to spend more time on, and which ones to let go.

The student evaluations did much of the same thing. The words again were very powerful. The students make a great argument for the value of this course.

Though the vast amounts of data I gathered will help Donna and me answer many important questions about our methods, I narrowed the action research questions to focus on how the course met our specific goals and objectives. I aimed to answer the following questions through action research:

- Can experiential group problem-solving and adventure activities build a classroom community, increasing a supportive, cohesive, emotionally safe school environment?

- Can adventure activities improve self-esteem?

- Should students be taught to belay? What is the value? Is it safe practice?

- Is experiential based adventure education an effective method for meeting the Wisconsin Model Academic Standards for Physical Education?

Here is how the evidence I found addressed those questions:

Can experiential-based group problem-solving and adventure activities build a classroom community, increasing a supportive, cohesive, emotionally safe school environment?
DATA: Journal Entries, Student Interviews, Audio Tape, Videotape, Photographs, Student Questionnaires

The evidence I gathered in my study affirms that these activities are very effective in developing a sense of camaraderie and cohesiveness between students in the group, as well as an emotionally and physically safe and supportive environment, and increased value of diversity and respect for others.

This conclusion is evidenced by the journal statements of all of the students in our class throughout the semester. It is demonstrated in their interactions with each other recorded in the audiotapes of classroom activities, and the video footage of students at work in the classroom. The student interviews also reflect the students' observations of the development of their classroom community. The photographs communicate the attentiveness, involvement, and respect for safety that our group demonstrated in their involvement in these activities. In the final student questionnaires that students completed as an evaluation of the course, students repeatedly reported about the sense of positive community that was developed in this class and their school.

Can adventure activities improve self-esteem?
Data: Journal Entries, Student Interviews, Audio Recording, Final Student Questionnaire

My analyses of the students' journals found repeated statements throughout the semester involving students' feelings of accomplishment, achievement, and success. Many students reported that they had done things they never thought they could. Some reported that they had grown and changed in positive ways. Many reported that they were proud of themselves and the class.

In the interview with our outside observer, Catherine Coberly, students reported that they had improved their ability to work with others and rely on themselves.

In reading the journals it appears that the self-esteem increase is directly related to the students' involvement in the high elements and belaying. Their involvement in the team problem-solving activities developed feelings of empowerment through leadership, and success in thinking of solutions to problems.

Should students be taught to belay? What is the value? Is it safe practice?
Data: Journal Entries, Student Interviews, Video Footage, Audio Recording, Belay Check-Off Sheets, Photographs, Outside Observer's Report, Student Questionnaires

The students' journal entries reflect how much they perceived that they gained from this experience. The entries describe their commitment to the safety of their peers, their sense of responsibility, and their focus. The entries describe the skills they are learning and their perceptions of the value of these skills. Repeatedly students report a sense of accomplishment and achievement through their experience as belayers.

Many students report that this training in belaying and climbing will lead to lifelong leisure skills. Some report that they have joined the local rock gym and have signed up for summer adventure programs.

The interview with Catherine Soberly also affirms the value and appropriate practice of belaying from the students' perspective.

The students' journal entries, their success in the belay training check-off, and the video footage and photos of the students attentively and safely belaying are all evidence of the that students are capable of appropriately managing belaying in this class (under our supervision). The observations of our outside observer also affirm this statement.

Is experiential-based adventure education an effective method for meeting the Wisconsin Standards for Physical Education?
Data: Journal Entries, Photographs, Video Footage, Audio Recording, Student Interviews, Student Questionnaires

All of the student journal entries were sorted and categorized by the specific Wisconsin Model Academic Standards for Physical Education. They addressed leading an active lifestyle and learning skills, specifically problem-solving, communication, physical skill development/health-enhancing fitness, and the value of diversity.

In my analyses of the students' journal entries, all focus areas of the Wisconsin Model Standards were touched upon through the classroom activities, and students report positive progress in each of these areas. It is clear that challenge course programs are valuable in meeting areas that are often difficult to reach in traditional physical education coursework, such as the value of diversity and the development of problem-solving and responsibility skills.

References

Anderson, G., Herr, K., & Nihlen A. (1994). *Studying your own school*. London: Sage Publications.

Benardete, S. (1984). *Commentary to Plato's theaetetus*. Chicago: University of Chicago Press.

Brain compatible strategies, (2004). San Diego, CA: The Brain Store.

Cain, J., Cummings, M., & Stanchfield J. (2005). *A teachable moment: A facilitator's guide to activities for processing, debriefing, reviewing and reflection*. Dubuque, IA: Kendall Hunt Publishing.

Curry, L. (1990). One critique of the research on learning styles. *Educational Leadership, 48*, 50-56.

Dewey, J. (1938). *Experience and education*. New York: Macmillan Publishing Co.

Dewey, J. (1933). *How we think*. Boston: D.C. Heath and Company Publishers.

Diamond, M., & Hobson, J. (1998). *Magic trees of the mind*. New York: Penguin Putnam.

Dunn, R., Dunn, K., & Price, G. E. (1984). *Learning style inventory*. Lawrence, KS: Price Systems.

Elliot, J. (1991). *Action research for educational change*. Philadelphia: Open University Press.

Fleugelman, A. (1976). *The new games book*. The New Games Foundation, Headlands Press.

Gardner, H. (1993). *Frames of mind: The theory of multiple intelligences*. New York: Basic Books.

Hendricks, G., & Ludeman, K. (1997). The corporate mystic: A guidebook for visionaries with their feet on the ground. New York: Bantam.

Jensen, E. (2000). *Brain-based learning*. San Diego, CA: The Brain Store.

Jensen, E. (1998). *Teaching with the brain in mind*. Alexandria, VA: Association for Supervision and Curriculum Development.

Kolb, D. (1984). *Experiential learning: Experience as the source of learning and development*. Upper Saddle River, NJ: Prentice Hall.

Luckner, J., & Nadler. R. (1997). *Processing the experience: Strategies to enhance and generalize learning (2nd Ed)*. Dubuque, IA: Kendall Hunt Publishing Company.

McDermott, J. (1973). *The philosophy of John Dewey*. Chicago: The University of Chicago Press.

Paley, V. (1992). *You can't say you can't play*. Cambridge: Harvard University Press.

Rohnke, K. (1989). *Cowstails and cobras II*. Dubuque, IA.: Kendal Hunt Publishing.

Rohnke, K. (1991). *Bottomless bag again*. Dubuque IA: Kendall Hunt Publishing.

Rohnke, K., & Butler, S. (1995). *Quicksilver*. Dubuque, IA: Kendall Hunt Publishing.

Rohnke, K., & Grout, J. (1998). *Back pocket adventure*. Needham Heights, MA: Simon & Schuster Education Group.

Sandelands, L. E. (1998). Feeling and form in groups. *Visual Sociology, 13(1)*, 5-23.

Schoel, J., Prouty, D., & Radcliffe, P. (1988). *Islands of healing*. Hamilton, MA: Project Adventure, Inc.

Schon, D.A. (1983). The Reflective Practitioner: How professionals think in Action. New York: Basic Books, Inc.

Simpson. S. (2001, February 16-18). *A continuum of processing techniques*. Paper presented as part of symposium on group facilitation at the annual TEAM conference, Chicago IL.

Simpson, S. (2003). *The leader who is hardly known: Self-less teaching from the Chinese tradition*. Bethany, OK: Wood 'N' Barnes Publishing.

Simpson, S., Miller D., & Bocher B. (2006). *The processing pinnacle: An educator's guide to better processing*. Bethany, OK: Wood 'N' Barnes Publishing.

Sousa, D. (2006). *How the brain learns*. Thousand Oaks, CA: Sage Publications.

Sugerman, D., Doherty, K., Garvey, D., & Gass, M. (2000). *Reflective Learning: Theory and Practice*. Dubuque, IA: Kendall Hunt Publishing.

Takahashi, S. (1995). Aesthetic properties of pictorial perceptions. *Psychological Review, 102(4)*, 671-683.

Wood 'N' Barnes Staff. (1998). *The me I see, 2E: Learning through writing and reflection*. Bethany, OK: Wood 'N' Barnes Publishing.

Resources

Jen Stanchfield's Experiential Tools
- Maker of Miniature Metaphors© processing kit
- A resource for
  - Postcard sets
  - Processing tools
  - Journals
  - Buttons
  - Pewter "found word" stones

www.experientialtools.com
jen@experientialtools.com

36 Merrill Mundell Rd, South Newfane, VT 05351
802-348-6390

Training Wheels Inc.
- Wide range of portable teambuilding activities
- Processing tools including:
  - Body Part Debrief™
  - The Community Puzzle
- Books
- Workshops

www.training-wheels.com
michelle@training-wheels.com

7095 South Garrison Street, Littleton, CO 80128
888-553-0147

The Institute for Experiential Education
Creators of participant-directed processing tools such as:
- Chiji Cards
- Pocket Processor
- Chiji Processing Dice

www.chiji.com

115 Fifth Avenue South, Suite 430, La Crosse, WI 54601
608-784-0789

Books for Facilitators/Community Building Activities

Activities that Teach by Tom Jackson. 2001, Red Rock Publishing, Cedar City, UT. 435-586-7058.

Adventure Play: Adventure Activities for Preschool and Early Elementary Age Children by Nancy Macphee Bower. 2002, Pearson Custom Publishing.

Back Pocket Adventure by Karl Rohnke and Jim Grout. 1998, Project Adventure, Hamilton, MA.

Book on Raccoon Circles by Jim Cain and Tom Smith. 2002, Learning Unlimited, Tulsa, OK.

Bottomless Bag Again by Karl Rohnke. 1994, Kendall Hunt Publishing, Dubuque, IA.

50 Ways to Use Your Noodle by Chris Cavert and Sam Sikes. 1997, Learning Unlimited, Tulsa, OK.

Funn Stuff by Karl Rohnke. 1995, Kendall Hunt Publishing, Dubuque, IA. .

Games (& other stuff) for Group, Book 1: Activities to Initiate Group Discussion by Chris Cavert and friends. 1999, Wood 'N' Barnes Publishing, Bethany, OK.

Games (& other stuff) for Teachers: Classroom Activities that Promote Pro-Social Learning by Chris Cavert, Laurie Frank, & friends. Wood 'N' Barnes Publishing, Bethany, OK.

Journey Toward the Caring Classroom: Using Adventure to Create Community in the Classroom. 1999, by Laurie Frank. 2004, Wood 'N' Barnes Publishing, Bethany, OK.

More Activities That Teach by Tom Jackson. 1995, Red Rock Publishing, Cedar City, UT. 435-586-7058.

More the Merrier: Lead Playful Activities with Large Groups by Sam Sikes, Faith Evans, and Chris Cavert. 2007, DoingWorks Publishing.

New Games Book by Andrew Fleugelman. 1976, The New Games Foundation, Headlands Press.

104 Activities That Build: Self-Esteem, Teamwork, Communication, Anger Management, Self-Discovery, Coping Skills by Alanna Jones. Rec Room Publishing, Richland, WA. 888-325-GAME.

Playing With a Full Deck: 52 Team Activities Using a Deck of Cards! by Michelle Cummings. 2007, Kendall Hunt Publishing, Dubuque, IA.

Quicksilver by Karl Rohnke and Steve Butler. 1995, Kendall Hunt Publishing, Dubuque, IA.

Still More Activities That Teach by Tom Jackson. 2000, Red Rock Publishing, Cedar City, UT. 435-586-7058.

Teamwork & Teamplay by Jim Cain and Barry Jolliff. 1998, Kendall Hunt Publishing, Dubuque, IA.

BOOKS FOR FACILITATORS/REFLECTION

Lasting Lessons: A Teacher's Guide to Reflecting on Experience by Clifford Knapp. 1992, ERIC Clearing House.

Me I See, 2E: Learning Through Writing and Reflection. 1998, Wood 'N' Barnes Publishing, Bethany, OK.

Metaphors for Living: Stories & Related Experiential Exercises for Individual, Group & Family Growth by Jackie Gerstein. 2002, Wood 'N' Barnes Publishing, Bethany, OK.

Open to Outcome: A Practical Guide for Facilitating & Teaching Experiential Reflection by Micah Jacobsen and Mari Ruddy. 2004, Wood 'N' Barnes Publishing, Bethany, OK.

Processing Pinnacle: An Educator's Guide to Better Processing by Steven Simpson, Dan Miller, and Buzz Bocher. 2006, Wood 'N' Barnes Publishing, Bethany, OK.

Processing the Experience: Enhancing and Generalizing Learning by John Luckner and Reldan Nadler. 1997, Kendall Hunt Publishing, Dubuque, IA.

Reflective Learning: Theory and Practice by Deborah Sugerman, Kathryn Doherty, Daniel Garvey, and Michael Gass. 2000, Kendall Hunt Publishing, Dubuque, IA.

Teachable Moment: A Facilitator's Guide to Activities for Processing, Debriefing, Reviewing and Reflection by Jim Cain, Michelle Cummings, and Jennifer Stanchfield. 2005, Kendall Hunt Publishing, Dubuque, IA.

EXPERIENTIAL EDUCATION PHILOSOPHY

Action Research for Educational Change by John Elliot. 1991, Open University Press, Philadelphia.

Conscious Use of Metaphor in Outward Bound by Steven Bacon. 1983, Colorado Outward Bound School, Denver, CO.

Ethical Issues in Experiential Education by Jasper Hunt. 2002, Kendall Hunt Publishing, Dubuque, IA.

Experience in Education by John Dewey. Collier Books, New York.

Experiential Learning: Experience as the Source of Learning and Development by David Kolb. 1984, Prentice-Hall, Englewood Cliffs, NJ.

How We Think by John Dewey. 1933, D.C. Heath and Company Publishers, Boston, MA.

Leader Who is Hardly Known: Self-less Teaching From the Chinese Tradition by Steve Simpson. 2003, Wood 'N' Barnes Publishing, Bethany, OK.

Philosophy of John Dewey by John McDermott. The University of Chicago Press, Chicago.

Studying Your Own School by Gary Anderson, Kathryn Herr, and Ann S. Nihlen. 1994, Corwin Press.

Teaching With the Brain in Mind by Eric Jenson. 2005, Association for Supervision & Curriculum Development.

You Can't Say You Can't Play by Vivian Paley. 1993, Harvard University Press, Cambridge, MA.

Index

About the Author

JEN STANCHFIELD, MS, began her professional involvement in experiential education in 1989. In her years as an educator, recreational therapist, and challenge course facilitator she has worked with many different groups of all ages and backgrounds from elementary students, to patients in treatment programs, to corporate executives. Jen earned her undergraduate degree at the University of New Hampshire in recreational therapy and outdoor education and a masters of science in experiential education from Minnesota State University at Mankato.

Through these experiences Jen has developed a repertoire of activities, tools, and tricks that she enthusiastically shares with other facilitators in her byline "Facilitator's Toolbox" and numerous conference presentations and workshops. A focus of her work has been developing reflective tools, and she is co-author of *A Teachable Moment: A Facilitator's Guide to Activities for Processing, Debriefing, Reviewing, and Reflection.*

Jen is currently principal of Experiential Tools, a consulting company that provides resources and training for educators. She works directly with students and teachers, and designs experientially based curriculum for schools, treatment programs, and other organizations. She and her husband Paul live in the mountains of Southern Vermont.

Contact Information and Workshops:
For Jen's Facilitation Tips & Tools and Workshops:
www.experientialtools.com
jen@experientialtools.com
802-348-7297